THE

COLD WAR

OTHER TITLES IN THE COMPACT GUIDE SERIES

Winston Churchill

DNA

The Elements

Queen Elizabeth II

The Napoleonic Wars

THIS IS AN ANDRE DEUTSCH BOOK

Text © Norman Friedman 2005, 2009
Design © Andre Deutsch 2019

Originally published in 2004 under the title
The Cold War Experience.

This edition published in 2019 by Andre Deutsch
A division of the Carlton Publishing Group
20 Mortimer Street
London
W1T 3JW

Typeset by JCS Publishing Services Ltd

Printed in Italy
A CIP catalogue for this book is available from the British Library

ISBN: 978-0-233-00591-1

THE
COMPACT
GUIDE

T H E

C O L D   W A R

Norman Friedman

ANDRE
DEUTSCH

C O N T E N T S

INTRODUCTION

The Cold War shaped our times. To fight it, the West created institutions such as the European Economic Community (since 1993 the European Union) and NATO. Both West and East suffered the consequences of pouring far more money into the military than might otherwise have been the case. Soviet science and technology were overwhelmingly designed to support a vast military machine, the sheer cost of which ultimately sank the country. Western science and technology were often driven by the need to maintain an edge over the Soviet Union, particularly after the Soviets demonstrated their own prowess with *Sputnik*, the first artificial satellite, in 1957. The computers which dominate our world exist because they were needed to fight the Cold War. The missiles created for the Cold War put men into space and revolutionized our world by launching satellites of various kinds. Even the terrorism which currently bedevils international harmony and co-operation can be traced back to tactics each side adopted to weaken the other during the Cold War.

What exactly was the Cold War? One definition would be that it was the West's long struggle to overcome the Soviet attempt to dominate it and the world. Another would be that it was the struggle for control of Europe. Some would see it as World War III, fought out in slow motion and with relatively little fighting. In this context wars like those in Korea and Vietnam were campaigns in the larger Cold War. Many expected the Cold War to turn into a full-scale World War III, but that never happened, largely because both sides feared nuclear war. That both sides so often had the sense to draw back from the brink is probably the most hopeful part of the story.

The roots of the war can be found in the ideology which shaped the Bolshevik Revolution at its formation in 1917. Lenin and his cohorts saw themselves primarily as world revolutionaries; inevitably, the established order would retaliate (such as when Britain, France, the United States and Japan intervened in the Russian Civil War in 1918–20). By the 1930s it seemed that the Soviets felt secure enough to be less hostile to the outside world. Joseph Stalin won power in the Soviet Union partly by arguing that effort should be concentrated on developing "socialism in one country", i.e., in the Soviet Union. It was his defeated rival, Leon Trotsky, who had called for focusing on revolution outside the Soviet Union.

For the West, the beginning of the Cold War was the discovery, after World War II, that Stalin had never abandoned his revolutionary roots; he still wanted to spread his system throughout the world. The policy difference with Trotsky had been no more than a device to gain power; once Stalin was in control, he felt free to change direction. Unlike a Western political party, the Soviet Communist Party followed whatever line he chose.

Norman Friedman

●

CHAPTER ONE

A FAILED

PEACE

Initially it seemed to many that the three victorious World War II powers – the United States, the United Kingdom and the Soviet Union – would co-operate to maintain the peace they had bought at so dreadful a cost in blood and money.

1945

4 February: Big Three leaders meet at Yalta to chart the post-war world; Stalin is asked to enter the Pacific War

25 April: United Nations founding conference meets in San Francisco

8 May: Germany surrenders, is occupied by US, British, French, Soviet forces

17 July: Big Three meet in Potsdam

6 August: Atomic bomb dropped on Hiroshima

8 August: Stalin enters the war against Japan as promised

2 September: Japan surrenders

1946

9 February: Stalin's speech revives pre-war claim that Communism and Capitalism are "incompatible" – in effect, end of the wartime truce

As the war was ending in February 1945, the victorious leaders met at Yalta in the Soviet Union. Among other things, Stalin agreed to hold free elections in Poland, which his armies had liberated (and occupied). A few months later the Allied leaders met at Potsdam in newly defeated Germany. Stalin had held the promised elections – but he had crudely rigged them in favour of the Communists, ending any hope of Polish democracy for over 40 years. The Western leaders protested, but they knew that they could not do anything. They still hoped that the Polish elections were an exception, made because Poland was particularly vital to the Soviets; it would be several years before they realized that Stalin's vision of a post-war world did not match theirs.

The victorious powers divided Germany into what they saw as four

---

Joseph V. Stalin (1879–1953)

Stalin rose to absolute power in the Soviet Union following Lenin's death in 1924; by 1936 he was in full control, eliminating all potential rivals in a series of staged trials. Although Lenin had created the system of concentration camps, under Stalin millions of people were imprisoned or shot. Millions of others died in famines he caused, particularly in Ukraine. Stalin justified his tyranny on the ground that it was necessary for the crash industrialization ("development in one country") needed for survival.

---

temporary occupation zones (American, British, French and Soviet) – which turned out to be the long-term focus of the Cold War. Although Berlin, the pre-war capital, lay deep inside the Soviet zone (which became East Germany), it too was divided into four zones, a fact which was later very significant. The powers agreed that elections would be held throughout Germany to form a reunified country. Gradually it

Sir Winston Churchill (1874–1965)

Churchill led Britain to victory in World War II. As a Cabinet Minister during and after World War I, he was involved in the British intervention against the Communists in the Russian Civil War. His long experience made him quite aware of just how hostile the Soviets could be; he was one of the first to see Stalin as a new Hitler. He saw in Stalin's death a possibility to end the Cold War, and to that end he helped arrange the 1955 summit between President Eisenhower and Khrushchev.

became clear that Stalin hoped to cause sufficient chaos in the non-Soviet zones to convince voters there to choose Communists, so that the whole country, the most industrialized in Europe, would fall into his hands. The British and the Americans reluctantly realized that unless they helped rebuild the parts of Germany they occupied, merely feeding the people there would be ruinously expensive. To that end they joined their zones, creating a new currency separate from that in the Soviet zone to the east – and the beginning of a new country, West Germany. Stalin saw the whole effort as concerted opposition to him. That initially made the French reluctant to join.

In many countries occupied by the Germans, Communists had been very prominent in the resistance and hence enjoyed considerable post-war prestige. Communist parties in France and in Italy were particularly powerful. Maurice Thorez, leader of the French Communists, told Stalin that it might soon be time for them to overthrow the French government. Stalin's own adviser, Ivan Maisky, had told him that the West would not resist as long as his men gained power in apparently democratic fashion. He revived a pre-war policy, the Popular Front, in which Communists were allowed to participate in Western governments (both France – in the 1930s – and Spain – during the Civil War – had had a Popular Front government). Presumably the hope was that a mixed government including Communists could be dominated by the Communist party. In theory, several of the post-war Communist governments of Eastern Europe were Popular Fronts, including minority puppet parties.

CHAPTER TWO

THE

IRON CURTAIN

Only gradually did it dawn on Western leaders that Stalin was hostile. Stalin considered World War II not a disaster, but a great opportunity; it had cleared "imperialism" from Central Europe.

1944

8 September: Communist coup in Bulgaria

1945

6 March: Communist regime installed in Romania

28 June: Communist "government of national unity" formed in Poland

4 November: Non-Communist party wins Hungarian election

1946

5 March: Winston Churchill delivers the "Iron Curtain" speech

26 May: Communists win plurality in Czechoslovakia; multi-party government

10 November: Communists are the largest party in the French assembly

1947

19 January: Rigged elections in Poland maintain Communist government

30 May: Communist coup in Hungary

1948

25 February: Communist coup in Czechoslovakia

He told a senior Yugoslav Communist, Milovan Djilas, that another war, perhaps in 10 or 20 years, might destroy imperialism altogether. Wherever the Soviet army was in occupation at the end of World War II, Stalin intended to maintain power. By early 1946 Soviet-occupied Poland, Bulgaria and Romania all had Communist governments. Communist guerrillas who had liberated Yugoslavia and Albania retained power in both. Soviet-occupied Hungary still had a semblance of democracy, but the Soviet army held real power. In a speech at Westminster College, Fulton, Missouri in March 1946, Winston Churchill declared that an "iron curtain has descended across the Continent", a metaphor earlier used by the journalist St Vincent Troubridge in October 1945. Stalin was little different from Hitler. Churchill's speech now seems to express perfectly what was happening, but it had a very cold reception at the time.

Until the West saw Stalin's efforts as a grab for power, there was a chance that Popular Front tactics would bring Communists to power outside Soviet-occupied Europe, most likely in France or in Italy. However, in 1947 the Soviets rigged the Hungarian election to bring Communists

Josip Broz Tito (1892–1980)
Tito led the guerrilla army which liberated Yugoslavia from the Nazis, and therefore enjoyed particular and independent prestige within the post-war Communist world. Stalin found this combination intolerable. He ejected Tito from the world Communist movement and ordered him killed. Tito's ejection (or defection) demonstrated that the Cold War was often more about Soviet imperialism than about ideology; he remained Communist but independent of Moscow. His other major achievement, now sadly evident, was to hold together the hostile ethnic groups of his country.

into control. That apparently convinced the French government that France had better resist Stalin; France had been allied to Hungary before World War II. Only pro-Soviet Czechoslovakia, which was not occupied, was still nominally free. In February 1948, however, Stalin ordered a coup there; mere friendliness was not enough. Eastern Europe was now a new Soviet empire. Its population was imprisoned behind a line of barbed wire, watchtowers and minefields – a physical iron curtain. Instead of independent governments, all the new Communist People's Republics were ruled by men chosen – and removed at will – by Moscow.

Finland was the only exception to Stalin's control over the countries his army had defeated or occupied during World War II. In defending their country, the Finns had inflicted eight times the losses on their Soviet invaders that they themselves had suffered, but, without outside military aid, had been compelled to sue for peace. In 1948 the Finnish Communists planned a Czech-like coup, but it was aborted when it became clear that there would be concerted resistance. Finland maintained its neutrality throughout the Cold War.

CHAPTER THREE

THE TRUMAN DOCTRINE, MARSHALL PLAN AND NATO

The US government hoped that the Europeans, led by the British, could handle Stalin largely by themselves.

1944

December: Greek Civil War breaks out; British back Greek government

1947

21 February: British tell Americans they will be stopping their funding of the Greek government

12 March: Truman announces Truman Doctrine

5 June: Marshall proposes Marshall Plan

2 July: Soviets reject Marshall Plan aid and force Eastern Europeans to do likewise

22 September: Soviets create COMINFORM to co-ordinate Communist regimes

1948

17 March: Treaty of Brussels: Western European Union formed

1949

24 August: NATO Treaty effective with accession of France

1955

9 May: West Germany joins NATO

14 May: Warsaw Pact (Communist military alliance) formed

US involvement might be limited to occupying parts of Germany and Austria. Americans grossly underestimated the damage World War II had done; Western Europe could not revive by itself. Stalin presented a double threat: his massive army might simply invade to install Communist governments, or the millions of hungry, disillusioned Europeans might vote in Stalin's Communists. Once in, the Communists would never leave peacefully.

In Greece, Communist guerrillas, supported by Marshal Tito's Yugoslavia, were fighting the Greek royalist government backed by the British. In 1947 the British shocked the Americans: they were too badly exhausted to stay in Greece. If the Communists won, the Soviets would gain Greek bases in the Mediterranean, threatening the tanker route from the Middle East to Western Europe.

For 150 years American governments had avoided peacetime entanglements in Europe. President Harry Truman remembered that the last such act of avoidance, after World War I, had probably helped cause World War II. He proclaimed the Truman Doctrine: the United States would help any country faced by Communist attack. American material aid would help keep Greece out of Stalin's hands. The involvement was

Harry S. Truman (1884–1972) and Ostpolitik

Truman replaced Walter Ulbricht because he accepted the West German opening to the East (Ostpolitik), which the Soviets considered useful. That required greater repression in East Germany; otherwise the population might come to expect freedom. In 1980 Honecker demanded a Czech-style invasion to put down the Polish Solidarity movement. In 1988 he rejected glasnost and perestroika. By the time Mikhail Gorbachev was visiting him for the 40th anniversary of East Germany, a coup to unseat him was already well advanced.

exactly what Stalin had hoped to avoid. The Soviet leader never forgave Tito for acting on his own. He ordered Tito assassinated and Yugoslavia invaded (neither of which happened). Tito befriended the West. This defection became Stalin's nightmare: the West could accept a Communist government as long as it was not tied to the Soviet Union.

The Americans recognized that Western Europe could never be secure unless its economies were revived. On 5 June 1947 Secretary of State George C. Marshall proposed the European Recovery Program, better known as the Marshall Plan. Aid was conditional on the Europeans developing a US-approved plan. The British were the first to welcome aid. US planners saw Western Europe as a single economic unit, and pressed for economic union; the Marshall Plan ultimately led to the current European Union. The Plan touched off the unprecedented post-war revival of Western Europe. It included West Germany, then occupied by the Americans, British and French. About $13 billion was provided in 1948–53. Stalin rejected the Marshall Plan (and ordered the Poles and the Czechs to do likewise). Czech interest showed him that he had insufficient control over their country; hence the February 1948 coup there. The coup dramatized the threat posed by large Communist parties in the West; the United States provided crucial aid which helped the Christian Democrats win the 1948 Italian elections against Communists backed by Stalin.

Sir Ernest Bevin (1881–1951)

Bevin became British Foreign Secretary with the Labour victory of 1945. He may have been chosen specifically because he was considered tough enough to deal with the Soviets (and with the left wing of the Labour Party, which was intensely pro-Soviet). Bevin was among the first to recognize the depth of Soviet hostility, and his goal was to bind the United States to Europe. Thus, he led in welcoming the Marshall Plan, and he was the key architect of the NATO alliance.

No single European country could defend against the huge Soviet machine. Although the traditionally isolationist United States would not initiate a defensive union, it might join a union already formed by the Europeans. Knowing this, the British Foreign Secretary, Ernest Bevin, initiated the formation of a Western European Union (Britain, France, Belgium, Luxembourg and the Netherlands). Once that had been created, in 1949 the Americans created the North Atlantic Treaty Organization from it (additional members were the United States, Canada, Denmark, Iceland, Italy, Norway and Portugal). The key pledge was that "an attack on one is an attack on all," but initially the main American contribution was plentiful supplies of surplus equipment. To revive European military industry the United States paid for local production of military equipment, such as the first jet fighters to be built in many European countries. The United States also funded much European military research and development, again as a way of reviving vital European industries.

CHAPTER FOUR

THE BERLIN AIRLIFT

By early 1948 the economy in the zones of Germany occupied by the British and the Americans was reviving; on 18 June they introduced a new currency to fight Stalin's attempt to cause runaway inflation throughout Germany.

1947

1 January: Bizonia formed: US and British unify their German occupation zones

1948

March: Gen Lucius Clay, US commander in Berlin, warns of impending war

18 June: Western powers introduce a new single currency in their zones

24 June: Stalin closes land access to Berlin

28 June: Airlift begins

1949

12 May: Stalin compelled to open land access; airlift successful

23 May: West German state proclaimed

30 September: Airlift officially ends after more than 275,000 flights

7 October: East German state proclaimed

Stalin's German Party leader, Wilhelm Pieck, warned that the projected October 1948 elections in Berlin would be disastrous for the Communists unless the Western Allies were ousted from the city. Stalin had leverage: everything consumed in the sectors of Berlin occupied by the Western powers – West Berlin – came either directly from the Soviet zone or by road, rail or canal from the Western-occupied parts of Germany. Stalin decided to show the West Berliners that the Western powers could not protect them. He began to restrict land access to the city; on 23 June 1948 electricity and all supplies from East Germany were cut off. The next day Stalin barred all road, barge and rail traffic from the Western zones. He declared that the Western powers no longer had any rights to administer their zones. West Berliners were offered supplies in East Berlin, on condition that they accepted Soviet authority. Stalin seemed to be willing to risk war; his Berlin blockade was the first serious global crisis of the Cold War.

The Western Allies rejected Stalin's demands. They kept West Berlin alive by supplying it by air. The airlift began on 28 June 1948, when 150 aircraft brought in 400 tons of supplies. By mid-July British and American aircraft were providing 2,750 tons per day. That rose to 4,500 and then to 5,600 tons per day, partly using the new Tegel airport built by the West Berliners. The Soviets ended the blockade on 12 May 1949. About 2.5 million tons were delivered, at a cost of 60 American and British aircrew who died in crashes.

The Berlin airlift showed many in Europe that the West was willing to stand up to Stalin, and it showed Berliners that the West would accept serious risks (like having aircraft shot down *en route*) for their sake. The crisis was so serious that it drove the British and the Americans into their first post-World War II joint military planning, for fear that war might really be imminent. In July 1948 the United States moved B-29 bombers to Britain, the first US bombers based there since World War II. The gesture was particularly significant because the B-29, which had dropped the atomic bombs on Japan in 1945, was considered an atomic bomber. However, those planes sent to Britain were not equipped to drop atomic bombs (as Stalin's spies probably told him). To the Soviets, the airlift demonstrated not only Western resolve, but also Western air power. Unknown to the West, the Soviets concluded that they could not shoot down the aircraft supplying West Berlin. Where cargo-carriers could go, so could bombers; Stalin ordered an urgent programme to develop new air defences for the Soviet Union.

CHAPTER FIVE

CHINA   AND

DECOLONIZATION

**The Cold War was also fought outside
Europe. Japanese victories in World War
II largely ejected the Europeans from their
Asian empires.**

1945

August–September:
Japanese
surrender, often to
local guerrillas

2 September: Ho
Chi Minh proclaims
Republic of
Vietnam

17 November:
Sukarno proclaims
Indonesian republic
(Dutch fight him)

1947

15 August: Indian
independence
proclaimed; first
major European
colony freed

1948

16 June: War
against British
breaks out in
Malaya

1949

1 October: Mao
Zedong proclaims
People's Republic
of China

1950

15 August:
Indonesian republic
proclaimed after
Dutch withdrawal

1954

7 May: French
defeated at Dien
Bien Phu in
Vietnam

1 November: War
against French
breaks out in
Algeria

1955

18 April: Non-
aligned movement
formed at
Bandung; China a
leading member

As in Europe, Communists had been heavily involved in resistance efforts, and at the end of the war they tried to seize power in places such as Malaya and Vietnam. European attempts to reoccupy their empires proved difficult, partly because World War II had proven so crippling and partly because the Japanese triumphs had destroyed so much of the prestige on which European power in Asia depended.

The same US government which was so intent on preventing Soviet empire-building in Western Europe tended to support decolonization in Asia. Thus, in 1949 it was American pressure which forced the Dutch to concede independence to Indonesia. It would be several more years before the US position swung more towards supporting what was left of the European empires, but the conflict between the American positions inside and outside Europe would help cause serious turmoil within the Western Alliance.

Another factor was China. While Stalin seized Central Europe, a civil war raged in China. In 1949, Mao Zedong's Communists won the war, to some extent with Soviet help. Partisans of his opponent, Chiang Kai-shek, claimed that the United States had not helped enough, and that at a key moment it had stopped Chiang's armies in the hope of brokering a

Sukarno (1901–1970)

Sukarno led Indonesia to independence from the Netherlands. Although nominally non-aligned, by 1964 he was so impressed by Communist successes in South Vietnam and in Laos that he thought Communism the wave of the future, and he moved towards an alliance with Mao. He publicly embraced his Communist party (the largest outside a Communist country), and he fought an undeclared war with Malaysia. Failure in that war and American support for South Vietnam encouraged the Indonesian Army to overthrow Sukarno in 1965 to forestall an expected Communist coup.

compromise settlement. Although China had never been a colony, the country had been forced to grant foreign powers such as Britain and Japan (and, to a lesser extent, the United States) humiliating concessions. Mao presented his victory as another form of decolonization. He claimed a kind of senior role among the independence movements and their successor governments. For the moment, Mao could help Communist-led independence movements in neighbouring countries, such as Vietnam.

In some ways Mao was like Tito, nominally loyal to the world

Mao Zedong (1893–1976)

Zedong led the Chinese Communists to victory in the Chinese Civil War (1946–49), and decided to enter the Korean War largely to cement that victory (anti-Communists would be seen as traitors). He was shocked when the Soviets did not look upon him as Stalin's natural successor. Mao thought China could be developed industrially simply by unleashing the people's political energy. The resulting disasters began with the "Great Leap Forward" (1958–61) and culminated in the Great Cultural Revolution (1966–71).

Communist movement, but with the sort of independent prestige Stalin feared and resented. Stalin seems to have been a less than enthusiastic backer; he hoped that Mao would not succeed completely in the civil war he was fighting. Once Mao had won, Stalin's problem was to make sure that he did not suddenly decide to abandon him in favour of the West – which could offer much more help in rebuilding China after the devastation of World War II and civil war.

CHAPTER SIX

MCCARTHYISM

**To many in the West, the Cold War seemed
to be a new kind of conflict, in which
shadowy, treacherous Communists in their
countries helped Stalin attack.**

1946

5 November:
Joseph McCarthy
elected to US
Senate

1947

21 March: Loyalty
investigations of US
government
employees
authorized

1948

2 August: Alger
Hiss publicly
accused of being a
Communist agent;
he denies it

1950

21 January: Hiss
convicted of perjury
by team led by
Richard Nixon

9 February:
McCarthy speech to
Republican women
in Wheeling, West
Virginia, begins his
rise to prominence

1951

29 March:
Rosenberg "atomic
bomb" spies found
guilty (arrested July
1950)

1953

12 October:
McCarthy accuses
US Army of treason

1954

December:
McCarthy censured
by Senate

Did treason explain why the United States was doing so little to stop Stalin? Surely he could not have developed his own atomic bomb (tested in August 1949, much earlier than expected) without having traitors supply the necessary plans. There was an element of truth in such ideas; the Soviets had penetrated the US government to some extent, but those charging treason grossly exaggerated what had happened. Unfortunately, much of the crucial evidence of treason (derived by code-breaking) could not be used. Hence the decades-long debates over the two most celebrated cases of the time, the Hiss Trial and the Rosenberg Trial.

Republican Senator Joseph McCarthy found the political opportunity too good to pass up. Beginning with a speech in 1950, he attracted enormous attention by charging that the Truman administration had not only bungled security investigations, it was actively harbouring Communists. Although entirely false, this charge was so sensational that it guaranteed attention. Constantly changing the number of supposed traitors, and without much evidence of any kind, McCarthy gained political prominence. The idea was not new, but McCarthy was a much more magnetic personality than other Republicans who had tried the tactic, and he was much more willing to make irresponsible charges –

Joseph McCarthy (1908–1957)

McCarthy adopted his trademark anti-Communism (in which he had previously had no interest) because by 1950 he had so little to show for three years in the Senate (Washington reporters had voted him the worst – most useless – Senator) and he had to face re-election in 1952. He was entirely without conscience or conviction. He is remembered for his blank sheet of paper, which he always claimed listed senior Communists in the US government – but which he never allowed anyone to read.

such as that Secretary of State George C. Marshall was a Communist agent who had "sold out" China a few years earlier. He levelled a similar charge against Secretary of State Dean Acheson, who had made an unfortunate speech in January 1950 placing Korea outside the line of vital US outposts in the Pacific (thus, it might be imagined, inviting the North Korean attack). Truman administration attempts to curb McCarthy generally failed, particularly as Americans became worried about the Soviet bomb and then about what seemed to be the beginning of a new World War in Korea.

Truman's successor, President Eisenhower, was unwilling to challenge McCarthy directly: he was too popular. McCarthy fell only because he could not restrain himself; in 1954 he attacked the senior US Army leadership (mainly to curry favour for his own junior aide, David Schine, who had been drafted) and he was censured by the Senate.

Richard M. Nixon (1913–1994)

Nixon was Eisenhower's Vice President and then President in 1969–74. He rose on the wave of anti-Communism which was also exploited by Joseph McCarthy, and his excesses made him an object of hate by liberals. His experience with President Eisenhower gave him unusually good insights into foreign affairs. His unique combination of those insights with impeccable conservative credentials made it possible for him to open relations with Mao's China. He was also too willing to use "dirty tricks" to undermine his political enemies. Revelations of his illegal political operations brought him down in the Watergate scandal.

That did not stop other US politicians from seeking publicity by investigating Communist subversion. For a time it became easy to destroy any reputation simply by charging that a person was – or had been – a Communist or sympathizer. This process is particularly remembered for its effect in Hollywood, where many refused to name Communists with whom they had worked. Those who had abandoned Communism, seeing in it Stalin's tyranny, could only clear themselves by informing on their friends, a horrible mirror of the Communist practice of forcing those in the Party to betray their friends outside. A "blacklist" kept many writers and producers out of work, except when they adopted aliases. The practice naturally bred corruption: "investigators" could be hired either to clear or to condemn anyone. Overall, the effect of the blacklist was ironic: those who had suffered from it became heroes, whatever their politics and whatever their willingness to follow a Communist line against US interests.

McCarthy's charges were so exaggerated and ultimately so clearly false and self-serving that in effect he made anti-Communism a bad joke to many Americans (though others continued to believe in him). That had major consequences for the Vietnam War.

CHAPTER SEVEN

THE KOREAN

WAR

**World War II left Korea divided between a
Soviet occupation zone in the north and a
US zone in the south.**

1949

15 January: US forces withdrawn from Korea

September: Kim Il-sung asks Stalin for permission to attack South Korea

1950

12 January: Secretary of State Dean Acheson places Korea outside vital US interests

17 January: Stalin approves invasion of South Korea

25 June: North Koreans invade South Korea

15 September: Inchon landing

1951

2 April: NATO military command formed (SHAPE); Eisenhower appointed as its chief, SACEUR (Supreme Allied Commander Europe)

1952

August: Mao asks Stalin to allow him to seek terms

1953

5 March: Stalin dies

27 July: Armistice in Korea

In January 1949 US troops were withdrawn from South Korea. Beginning in 1949, the Communist ruler in the north, Kim Il-sung, asked Stalin to allow him to overrun his rival in the south. Given very limited resources, in January 1950 the American Secretary of State announced that Korea was outside the American defensive line in the Pacific. A few days later Stalin agreed to Kim's request, providing him with the tanks he used to invade South Korea on 25 June 1950.

General Douglas MacArthur (1880–1964)

MacArthur, commanding US occupation forces in Japan, became commander in Korea. By turns grossly over- and under-confident, MacArthur argued that once the Chinese entered the war he could not win it unless he could attack China itself. Fired for insubordination (President Truman refused to expand the conflict), MacArthur argued that the Far East (i.e., himself) rather than Europe should be the focus of the Cold War. He sought but failed to get the 1952 Republican Presidential nomination.

To many in the West, it seemed that the attack was the opening move in a third World War. The fact that Stalin had allowed his proxy to attack suggested that more moves might follow, for example an East German attack against West Germany. The US government moved in troops and asked the United Nations to authorize action. The Soviet delegation had earlier walked out in a dispute over whether to recognize Mao as the legitimate ruler of China. In its absence, the UN authorized the use of force – for the only time during the Cold War, so that the war became a United Nations operation, albeit dominated by the United States. Other countries supplying forces were Australia, Belgium, Canada, Colombia,

Ethiopia, France, Greece, the Netherlands, New Zealand, the Philippines, South Africa, Turkey, Thailand and the United Kingdom.

The North Korean offensive stalled outside the South Korean port of Pusan. The United States retained command of the surrounding sea; and in September 1950 its forces landed at Inchon, far behind North Korean lines. The North Korean force collapsed; for a time it seemed that North Korea itself would succumb. UN forces pushed deep into the country. Then, in November 1950, the Chinese entered the war, reversing the situation. By January 1951 the war had stalled near the original line between the two Koreas. Truce talks began, but the war continued until July 1953. As a measure of the scale of the war, 5.7 million Americans served and 54,246 died. The Chinese deployed more than two-thirds of their army and about half their air force; 148,400 died. Current estimates place the total cost of the war, to combatants and civilians, at 2 million dead.

The Soviet MiG-15 Fighter

This was the great surprise of the Korean War. In many ways it was as good as the US F-86 Sabre. It was powered by a copy of a British engine sold in 1946 by a British government still uncertain that it was really at war with the Soviets. The United States offered a huge reward to the first North Korean pilot who would defect with one.

Because Westerners saw Korea as the first phase of a larger war, the Cold War became a much more military confrontation. The United States expanded its military budget seven-fold specifically to prepare for the big war. Britain rearmed, and the European NATO countries were encouraged to build up their own forces. NATO soon turned to Germany to help defend itself, first by providing industrial might and then, beginning in 1955, with an army. In response, the Soviets formed their East European satellite countries into another alliance, the Warsaw Pact. The Soviets established the Warsaw Pact in May 1955, comprising Albania, Bulgaria, Czechoslovakia, East Germany (the German

Democratic Republic or GDR, also known by its German initials, DDR), Hungary, Poland, Romania and the Soviet Union. The great difference between the two alliances was that NATO was voluntary, each member retaining its own military command structure. The Warsaw Pact was completely subordinate to the Soviets, to the extent that the only command lines ran to its headquarters in Moscow.

CHAPTER EIGHT

T H E   B O M B

There is evidence that Stalin really was
thinking of following the Korean attack
with an attack in Europe. He may have
been deterred by the quick response in
Korea, but there was another reason no
European war ever broke out: the atomic
(and then the hydrogen) bomb.

1945

16 July: First
nuclear test,
Alamogordo

6 August: First
nuclear attack,
Hiroshima

1946

1 July: First
peacetime atomic
test, Bikini Atoll

1949

29 August: First
Soviet atomic bomb
tested

1950

May: Development
of a US tactical
atomic bomb
ordered

1952

1 November: First
H-bomb test, by the
US

1954

April: Storage of US
nuclear weapons
abroad (in Britain
and Morocco)
approved

14 May: Test of first
US deliverable
H-bomb

June: Storage of
US nuclear
weapons in
Germany approved

1961

31 October: Soviets
test largest
H-bomb in history

For the first time, not only people, but also their rulers realized that they might well be destroyed at the outset of a war. Widely publicized civil defence measures only reminded populations on both sides of how devastating the new threat was.

The bomb so outclassed all other weapons that it and its carriers became the main measure of military power. The British developed their own bomb because without one Britain could no longer be considered a major power. By the mid-1950s France, too, was working towards a nuclear bomb, for much the same reason.

Worse was to come, however. In the 1950s, first the United States and then the Soviet Union learned to build hydrogen bombs a thousand times more powerful than the original atomic bombs. One bomb could destroy an entire city. Atomic bomb power was measured in thousands of tons (kilotons) of TNT, as in the roughly 20 kilotons of the Hiroshima bomb. Early models could be carried only by large bombers such as a B-29 or B-47, but by the mid-1950s fighter-bombers could deliver their successors. Hydrogen bomb power was measured in millions of tons (megatons); a typical strategic bomb of the 1960s was one to two megatons (later weapons were smaller, as this sort of power was not necessary).

Nikita Khrushchev (1894–1971)

Khrushchev rose from pipe fitter to senior official by the late 1930s, partly thanks to Stalin's massive purges. After Stalin died, he was unusual among the Soviet hierarchy in retaining a belief in the potential of Communism (the others had become far more cynical). In turning the Soviet military towards missiles and nuclear weapons, he became the last Soviet leader to rein in Soviet military industry (he cancelled programmes to make way for new ones). That was probably the sin for which he was dismissed.

Boeing's Graceful B-47

This was the standard US atomic bomber of the mid-1950s. To fuel it in flight, Boeing developed the jet tanker which was modified to become the first successful commercial jet airliner, the Boeing 707. Rocket-assisted takeoff was invented to get the bomber off the ground ahead of an enemy strike: through the 1950s and 1960s the central question was whether one side or the other could save itself by striking first.

War with such weapons made very little sense. The Soviet leader of the mid-1950s, Nikita Khrushchev, had been raised on the idea that war between Capitalism and Communism was inevitable. When he saw the films of the first Soviet hydrogen bomb test, he could not sleep for days: it seemed that the world was finished. Then he realized that the bomb was an opportunity, not an end: there could be no central war between the two sides, but fighting by Communists for power in the Third World would not risk a nuclear response from the West. He began to ship arms to Third World governments and to revolutionaries. Within the Soviet Union, he paid for a bomb and missile programme by drastically cutting both his conventional forces and the production of their weapons. That made it possible for him to claim, deceptively, that he was disarming, but it also earned him the enmity of the officers he retired and of the industrialists whose plants he realigned. They ousted him, largely in retaliation, in 1964.

CHAPTER NINE

EXPLOSIONS IN EUROPE:

UPRISINGS IN THE GDR AND POLAND

Stalin died on 5 March 1953. People throughout the Soviet empire hoped the harsh conditions might be relaxed.

1953

5 March: Stalin dies

16 June: Rioting in East Berlin

27 June: Beria falls as result of uprising (he is shot in December)

1954

October: Khrushchev visits China alone (i.e., by this time he was in power)

1955

15 May: Soviets and Western powers withdraw from occupation of Austria

1956

28 June: Riots in Poznan, Poland demand lower food prices and end of Communist rule

19 October: Władysław Gomułka becomes Polish leader

When the Soviet government in East Germany demanded that they work harder, East German workers called a general strike. In June as many as 100,000 East Berlin workers rioted; this was the first major outbreak in Eastern Europe. Stalin's heirs decided that their choice was either to stay in East Germany by force or to abandon it, after which they might well be thrown out of the rest of Eastern Europe. They fought: two armoured divisions plus infantry went into East Berlin. Martial law was declared; the riots were suppressed. In East Berlin, 25 demonstrators were killed and another 378 injured; as many as 25,000 may have been arrested throughout East Germany. Of the 109 killed across the country, 41 were Soviet troops shot for refusing to shoot demonstrators. The disaster in East Berlin destroyed Stalin's first heir, his secret police chief, Lavrentiy Beria, who had advocated relaxing rule in East Germany. Among the other consequences were that the Soviets abandoned plans to use East German industry to produce weapons such as submarines for them.

Beria's successor, Nikita Khrushchev, realized that without some relaxation, at least inside the Soviet Union, the country would stagnate. Also, that by attacking Stalin he could destroy his own (Stalinist) political rivals. In February 1956 he denounced Stalin's crimes in a secret speech to a packed audience at the Twentieth Congress of the Communist Party. In effect, he admitted that the Soviet Union had been built on terror, with Stalin exploiting an illegal "cult of personality". The symbolic end of Stalinism was to remove Stalin's body from the tomb it had shared with Lenin's. However, once Khrushchev was gone in 1964 quiet attempts began to resurrect Stalin's memory.

Throughout the Communist world, Stalin's word had been law. Now that Khrushchev had replaced Stalin, the new Party line was that no national leader should rule as a god. That infuriated Mao, who had a cult of personality of his own. The same logic suggested that the men Stalin had installed throughout Eastern Europe were no longer legitimate. Rioting broke out in Poznan, Poland, in June 1956. In October the Polish Communist Party felt emboldened to replace Stalin's man, Boresław Bierut, with Władysław Gomułka. The latter had spent the war in Poland rather than safe in Moscow, and Stalin had purged him. Khrushchev

Władysław Gomułka (1905–1982)
Gomułka led the Polish Communists immediately after World War II, but was dismissed in 1948 on Stalin's orders for his potential independence (he was later imprisoned). The Poles thus considered him their man rather than Moscow's. Brought back in 1956, Gomułka managed a programme of limited liberalization. By 1970 it had exhausted its potential, and he had to reduce wages. He was ousted after rioting, which was the beginning of the cycle leading to the rise of Solidarity.

rejected Gomułka. As Stalin's heir, surely it was for him to choose his puppets throughout Eastern Europe.

The Poles threatened to use their own army to fight if the Soviets invaded. Poland was certainly vital to the Soviets; it was the route between Russia and the vital army in East Germany. Khrushchev backed off. The Poles had gained a small but significant measure of independence. For the first time, the Soviets realized that they lacked total control of their empire. Crucially the new Polish leader understood his own limits.

CHAPTER TEN

EXPLOSIONS IN

EUROPE:

HUNGARIAN UPRISING

In July 1956, presumably to forestall a crisis like that in Poland, the Soviets forced the Stalinist ruler of Hungary, Mátyás Rákosi, out of office.

1956

25 February: Khrushchev denounces Stalin and Stalinism: the "Secret Speech"

21 October: Hungarians demand removal of Soviet troops

23 October: Demonstrations begin Hungarian Revolution; Imre Nagy becomes premier

28 October: Official Hungarian demands for removal of Soviet troops

30 October: Nagy proclaims multi-party system

1 November: Nagy proclaims neutralist stance

4 November: Khrushchev sends in his tanks

7 November: Soviets gain control of Budapest and other cities

23 November: Soviets kidnap Nagy, violating safe conduct

1958

16 June: Nagy executed

Imre Nagy, a former premier imprisoned by Rákosi, was freed, along with many other political prisoners. The Hungarians were emboldened by the Polish success in bringing Gomułka to power. Massed demonstrators demanded that Nagy be appointed premier. Others called for Soviet troops to leave the country, and in one city the Hungarian secret police were attacked. Street fighting broke out across the country, and in Budapest a massive statue of Stalin, the symbol of Soviet power, was toppled. To calm the situation, the Hungarian Central Committee made Nagy premier, although a Stalinist, Ernő Gerő, retained real power as First Secretary of the Party. He called on the Soviets to crush the unrest, and Soviet tanks fought in Budapest and other Hungarian cities. Poland's Gomułka, who had barely avoided having the Soviets invade his own country, urged the Soviets to withdraw their troops. For a few days it seemed that they were doing so and that the Hungarians had won. Nagy found himself pressing for more and more radical measures: a multi-party system and then a neutralist foreign policy. Khrushchev could tolerate none of this. Negotiations camouflaged a massive build-up of Soviet tanks, which soon subdued Hungary. Nagy and his defence minister, Pál Maléter, were lured from a neutral embassy, arrested, and hanged. About 20,000 Hungarians were killed. Tens of thousands more were arrested.

The Hungarians called for help. However, President Eisenhower told his National Security Council that even rolling the Soviets back from Eastern Europe, which had long been a US goal, would not gain security for Western Europe, because the Soviets would still have nuclear weapons capable of devastating it from Soviet soil. After the failed uprising, some said that the US-sponsored radio stations (Radio Free Europe and Radio Liberty) had falsely promised armed help. Americans involved in the roll-back effort were disgusted by their government's failure to act. In the end, all that the revolutionary Hungarian government could do was open the border to Austria, allowing about 250,000 people to flee to the West.

The lesson seemed to be that resistance to Soviet rule was basically pointless. However, the Soviets drew a less optimistic lesson. They concluded that continued rule in Central Europe required carrots as well

Imre Nagy (1896–1958)

Nagy was a Hungarian Communist initially ejected from government in 1948 (as a possible Titoist) for protesting against forced collectivization of farms. Brought back at Khrushchev's insistence after Stalin's death, he pressed for liberalization, and was expelled again in 1955 for "Titoism". That made him a symbol of Hungarian independence, installed again as premier at popular insistence in 1956. In effect he was swept up in the Hungarian Revolution. Despite a safe conduct, he was arrested by the Soviets and executed after a secret trial.

as sticks. A quarter of a century later the cost of the carrots would help break the Soviet system. In Hungary itself, so much of the population had clearly sided with the rebels that the government the Soviets installed felt compelled to try to reconcile them. Its slogan became "anyone who is not against us is with us". By the 1980s the Hungarians were more willing than any other government in the Soviet bloc to experiment with innovations such as private enterprise.

CHAPTER ELEVEN

SPLITS IN THE FACADES

At first the Cold War seemed to be about a unified West facing a unified Communist world, but within a decade both camps were themselves split. In each case the interests of the leading power conflicted with those of the others in its group. In the West, the Americans still rejected what they saw as European colonialism.

1956

25 February: Khrushchev denounces Stalin (the "Secret Speech") and infuriates Mao

5 November: British and French attack Egypt at Suez

1958

1 June: Charles de Gaulle becomes French Premier (elected President 21 December)

August: Khrushchev fails to back Mao in Formosa Straits crisis

1960

1 August: Last Soviet advisers leave China

1962

1 July: France withdraws from Algeria

1964

16 October: First Chinese nuclear bomb test: insurance against Soviets

1966

30 June: De Gaulle announces that France will leave NATO military structure

1969

2 March: Battle on the Ussuri River

1979

27 February: China invades Vietnam, then a Soviet ally

In July 1956 the Egyptian dictator Gamal Abdel Nasser seized the Suez Canal, control of which the British and the French regarded as absolutely vital to their economic interests. The French believed that Nasser's support was maintaining a rebellion against them in Algeria. The United States had rejected their claim that parts of Algeria were integral to France and thus came under the NATO pledge of assistance. Nasser had been emboldened by Soviet support, including large arms shipments (which threatened the Israelis). The Israelis agreed to attack Egypt, providing the British and French with a pretext for intervention there in November 1956 (to protect the Canal).

Charles de Gaulle (1890–1970)

De Gaulle led the Free French during World War II and also the first post-war French government. Retiring in 1946, he was brought back in 1958 specifically to solve the Algerian problem. His larger objective was to restore the prestige ("grandeur") of France despite the loss of her empire and her limited economic power. Among his tools were the French nuclear force and a close alliance with Germany and the French nuclear force. He tried to eject the United States (and, to some extent, Britain) from Europe, withdrawing France from the military component of NATO.

US intervention saved Nasser. Hopes that the US role would be appreciated throughout the Third World proved futile. Nasser's own prestige soared and his association with the Soviets deepened as they replaced the arms destroyed in the war. The French concluded that the United States was an unreliable ally. By this time war in Europe was unlikely because both sides had so many nuclear weapons; the French could afford to weaken their alliance with the Americans. A decade later

France withdrew from the NATO military structure, although remaining a NATO member. Periodically the French tried to persuade the West Germans to do the same.

Dwight D. Eisenhower (1890–1969)

He was the first military commander of NATO and then US President (1953–61). Unique among modern American Presidents for his military experience (as Commander in Chief in Europe in 1944–45), he shaped the policy of nuclear deterrence, arguing that nuclear weapons made war in Europe unwinnable, hence pointless. The military side of the Cold War would be fought out in the Third World, often by irregular forces. Understanding that the Cold War would likely last many decades, he resisted buying excessively expensive new weapons, for the war he doubted would ever come.

In the Communist world, Mao Zedong feared that Khrushchev would sacrifice him to avoid nuclear war. The point seemed proven when he failed to support Mao against the United States in the attacks in 1958 against the Nationalist-held islands of Quemoy and Matsu. Khrushchev reneged on a promise to give the Chinese their own atomic bomb, then visited the United States before attending the celebration in 1959 of the tenth anniversary of the People's Republic. Given Mao's growing enmity, in 1960 the Soviets pulled their advisers from China, helping to block Chinese military modernization. Mao loudly derided Khrushchev as too cowardly to support him, or any other Communist facing the West. The charge was effective because much of Khrushchev's power derived from his position at the head of a "world revolutionary movement". Suddenly

Khrushchev badly needed allies like the East European Communist chiefs, and he had to bribe them to stay loyal.

The Soviets began to fear that the Chinese would join forces with the Americans. Shorn of their alliance with the Soviets, they might well assert their old claims to vast lands Russia had taken over during the past three centuries. In the late 1960s the Soviets floated rumours that they were seeking American approval for a pre-emptive attack on Chinese nuclear production facilities as a way of warning the Chinese off. Meanwhile they built a huge army on the Chinese border, at the expense of their forces in Europe. When the Soviets invaded Czechoslovakia in 1968, Mao feared that China might be next. To head that off, in March 1969 he had his troops ambush Soviet troops on Zhenbao (Damansky) Island in the Ussuri River on the Sino-Soviet border. Three years later he welcomed President Richard Nixon to Beijing. Because Soviet forces facing the Chinese could not threaten Europe, in the 1980s NATO countries made a concerted effort to provide the Chinese with the new military technology they needed.

CHAPTER TWELVE

SECRET

SERVICES: EAST

With conventional warfare all but ruled out by the bomb, both
sides emphasized espionage and unconventional operations. To
the Soviets, a single secret service, ultimately the KGB, was the
"sword and shield" of the ruling Communist Party, shielding
it from enemies at home, attacking enemies abroad both by
stealing their secrets and by conducting special operations.

1917

20 December:
Cheka (Soviet
secret service)
created

1933

1933–35:
"Cambridge Five"
recruited: Blunt,
Philby, Burgess,
MacLean,
Cairncross

1941

August: John
Cairncross tells
Soviets the British
are developing an
atomic bomb

1943

1943–45: Soviets
penetrate US
atomic bomb
project, gaining key
information

1945

5 September: Igor
Gouzenko defects

1946

3 February: First
publication of
Gouzenko
revelation of extent
of Soviet spying in
North America

1949

"Kim" Philby
arrives in
Washington as MI6
representative

1951

25 May: Guy
Burgess and
Donald MacLean
flee England

1983

1983–85: Treachery
by Aldrich Ames
leads Soviets to
eliminate major US
spy ring

1985

20 May: John
Walker arrested

The KGB led a string of sister services in the Eastern European countries, providing the Soviet government with a second line of control throughout Eastern Europe. These services were generally more closely connected to the KGB than to their own governments. Some of them were also much more paranoid: a sixth of the East German population worked for the Stasi, most of them as informers. The other East European security agencies were the Bulgarian DS, the Czech StB, the Hungarian AVB, the Polish SB and the Romanian DIE. In each case there was also a domestic police agency with its own intelligence arm. Thus the Soviets had the MVD. In East Germany the foreign arm was the HVA, Stasi being the domestic organization. In Romania the domestic security organization was the Securitate.

At the outset, the Soviets enjoyed the services of traitors, some of them highly placed, who had joined their cause for ideological reasons. Their most spectacular success was to steal most of the information the Soviets then used to build their own atomic bomb. Soviet spies recruited in Britain included H. A. R. ("Kim") Philby of the British MI6 intelligence service. As the MI6 representative in the United States in 1949–50 he was privy to nuclear secrets, probably including the (very small) number of US atomic bombs.

H. A. R. ("Kim") Philby (1912–1988)

Recruited by the Soviets at Cambridge in 1933, Philby later joined the British foreign intelligence service, MI6. As chief of its anti-Soviet section, he aborted the defection (to Britain) of at least one senior Soviet officer. In 1949 he became MI6 representative to Washington and likely future head of the service. Investigation for this promotion raised questions; the British may have used Philby to feed  misinformation back to Moscow. After Burgess and MacLean fled, he was limited by MI6 to part-time work. He escaped to Moscow in 1963.

Markus Wolf (1923–2006)

Wolf was the founder and long-time chief of the East German foreign intelligence agency. He was enormously successful in running agents in West Germany, as the West Germans tended to embrace those who had apparently chosen to escape the East. Perhaps his greatest success was inserting Günter Guillaume as Willy Brandt's personal assistant, privy to West German (and often to Western) policy-making. Brandt was Chancellor of West Germany at the time. Wolf retired in 1987, but he was probably involved in the final East German coup.

Late in 1945 Igor Gouzenko, a code clerk in the Soviet Ottawa Embassy, defected, revealing the extent of Soviet espionage. Many of the American spies were deactivated for fear of compromising their handlers. Khrushchev's revelations in 1956 about Stalin seem to have ended the era of ideologically motivated spies in the West. The Soviets did, however, continue to enjoy some notable successes. For example, in 1968 James Walker, an American naval code clerk, walked into their Washington Embassy, with spectacularly bad results for the United States. Code-breaking based on Walker's efforts was credited with ruining several operations in Vietnam, and it probably explains why so many US ballistic missile submarines unexpectedly encountered Soviet warships. More than a decade later Aldrich Ames, a disaffected middle-level CIA officer, single-handedly betrayed numerous American spies in the Soviet Union. Both the Walker and the Ames cases revealed the impotence of US counter-intelligence.

Like their Western rivals, the Soviets also developed intelligence technology. For example, they learned how to tap into the microwave repeaters used to transmit telephone messages across the United States.

When that was discovered in the late 1970s, signs suddenly blossomed all over government offices in Washington, warning of the need to be careful on the telephone.

Stasi "Smell Jars"

The Stasi was the East German internal security service. Its obsessive desire to know what every East German was thinking led it to force at least 400,000 (of a total population of 16 million) East Germans to inform on their friends and neighbours. To make it easier for its dogs to trail and attack its enemies, the Stasi maintained a library of "smell jars", compiled on the theory that its prospective enemies would sweat recognizably when being interrogated (in the knowledge that they might soon be tortured or imprisoned in the Stasi's concentration camps).

Perhaps the greatest difference between Soviet and Western intelligence was that the Soviets relied on theirs to copy their enemies' technology: their leaders believed profoundly that Western technology was better. Thus, when their own scientists told them that the Reagan administration "Star Wars" programme was unworkable, they still demanded a Soviet equivalent: if the Americans said they could do it, surely it could be done. This futile effort helped bankrupt the Soviet Union, and thus helped the Soviets lose the Cold War. The Reagan administration reportedly concocted other secret projects it knew violated laws of physics, hoping that the Soviets would steal the designs and then go broke trying to make them work.

CHAPTER THIRTEEN

SECRET

SERVICES: WEST

Unlike the Soviets, Western countries generally separated foreign intelligence services from domestic (defensive) ones. Code-breaking agencies, which were probably much more important in Britain and in the United States, were also separate.

1943

November: First intercepts of Venona traffic

1949

10 May: First recorded overflight of Soviet Union by US Air Force, to find supposed bomber bases

1954

FBI recruits Morris Childs

1955

February: US and Britain tap Soviet military telephone system in Berlin

4 August: First flight of U-2

1956

2 July: First U-2 mission over the Soviet Union

1960

Oleg Penkovsky offers his services to CIA

1 May: Gary Powers shot down in U-2; Paris summit conference wrecked

12 August: First photographs recovered from reconnaissance satellite

1963

11 May: Penkovsky convicted and sentenced to death

1970

Early 1970s: US taps Soviet underwater cable used by Pacific Fleet

The British services, MI5 (domestic) and MI6 (foreign), were both set up before World War I. The code-breaking organization, GCHQ, was a product of that war. The United States created its first unified intelligence service, the Office of Strategic Services (OSS), during World War II, with much input from MI6. The domestic agency, the FBI, already existed, a product of the "Red Scare" immediately after World War I. OSS was shut down after World War II, but in 1947 a new Central Intelligence Agency (CIA) was created. The US code-breaking agency, NSA, was created at the same time. Other Western countries, such as France, generally had similar organizations.

During the Cold War, the West found it difficult to maintain spies, partly because the closed Soviet society was very good at catching them. In the wake of disastrous penetrations such as "Kim" Philby, both the CIA and MI6 spent much of their time trying to make sure that they were not still being penetrated. The CIA's mole hunt was closed down because it was so destructive. Then counter-espionage was virtually abandoned, with the result that Aldrich Ames could operate unhindered. Even so, there were some striking successes. Soviet society was so badly distorted that senior officers such as Colonel Oleg Penkovsky of Soviet military intelligence offered their services from time to time. Penkovsky's insights into Soviet rocket tactics were vital in understanding what was happening during the Cuban Missile Crisis, but he was caught and executed soon after.

Oleg V. Penkovsky (1919–1963)

A senior military intelligence officer, he approached the British (after the Americans rejected him). Penkovsky was responsible for scientific intelligence, which the Soviets often used as the basis for industrial programmes. To see what was needed, he was made privy to many of the advanced Soviet military programmes. His insights were particularly important during the Cuban Missile Crisis. Penkovsky also provided copies of the Soviet military magazines describing Khrushchev's new nuclear-oriented strategy – which he considered so abhorrent that he turned spy. Penkovsky was tried and executed for espionage in 1963.

Perhaps the least-known but most striking US success was that of Morris Childs ("Solo"). In 1954 the FBI turned Childs, the badly disaffected number-two man in the US Communist Party. Because they acted as though each country's Communist Party was that country's future government, the Soviets treated Childs as they would a foreign minister, making him privy to their policy decisions. Childs became personally friendly with the senior Chinese leadership, so the Soviets used him as a go-between in attempts to patch up the Sino-Soviet split. Unfortunately no one at the CIA could believe that the FBI could produce an agent this good, so it was some considerable time before Childs's remarkable material was used – after which it was eagerly devoured in Washington.

Given very limited ability to penetrate the closed Soviet society, the West concentrated on developing some remarkable intelligence-gathering systems, beginning with high-altitude aircraft such as the U-2, and then following up with large numbers of satellites of various types. In this it helped that the West had a much better industrial base. Much effort also went into code-breaking, although it is still difficult to say how successfully (the Soviets were good at code security). One success is known: Venona. During World War II the Soviets had slipped in the way they protected communications with their agents, and Venona was the decades-long attempt to break messages this compromised. It revealed many of the Soviet agents who were caught in the 1940s and early 1950s, such as the Rosenbergs and Alger Hiss. Ironically, the Soviets were tipped off to the early successes of the Venona project by their own agent within the US code-breaking organization (and by Philby); they were presumably less aware of later successes.

Francis Gary Powers (1929–1977)

Powers flew the U-2 shot down by the Soviets on May Day 1960. He survived to be placed on trial in Moscow. He was sentenced to three years of prison and seven years of hard labour, but on 10 February 1962 he was exchanged for "Rudolf Abel" (actually KGB Col. Vilyam Fisher) in Potsdam. He served as a test pilot for Lockheed, which built the U-2, in 1963–70 and later died in a helicopter accident, while a radio traffic-reporter.

CHAPTER FOURTEEN

S P U T N I K
A N D   T H E
M I S S I L E   A G E

Until 1957 Westerners generally saw the Soviet Union as the country capable of fielding a mass army (the old "Russian steamroller") with tens of thousands of tanks, but not of developing sophisticated aircraft and electronics.

1957

26 August: Soviets launch world's first ICBM

4 October: Soviets launch *Sputnik*

3 November: Soviets launch first living thing into space, "dog Laika"

1958

31 January: First successful US satellite launch

1961

12 April: Yuri Gagarin becomes first man to orbit the earth

1961 (ctd)

5 May: Alan Shepard becomes first US man in space (sub-orbital mission)

25 May: President Kennedy announces goal of placing a man on the moon within the decade

1963

26 July: First communications satellite in orbit

1969

21 February: Failure of massive Soviet N-1 rocket dooms Soviet moon effort

20 July: US astronauts land on the moon

This image had been shaken only slightly by the sudden appearance in Korea of the MiG-15 jet, which outperformed existing Western fighters. On 4 October 1957, however, the Russians launched *Sputnik*, the first artificial earth satellite. American attempts to put into orbit Explorer, a much smaller satellite, failed dramatically as rocket after rocket exploded on the launch pad. In Europe, the NATO allies began to wonder whether the American military technology on which they were relying to defend themselves was really as superior as they had imagined. The small sphere beeping as it passed around the earth seemed to be mocking the West.

Sputnik was the beginning of a scientific race, mainly a space race, which culminated in the American moon landing a little more than a decade later. *Sputnik* itself was not, of course, a weapon, but the rocket which launched it was a modified intercontinental ballistic missile (ICBM). In effect the *Sputnik* success proved that the missile worked. Up to that time, bombs, however horrific, had been delivered by bombers, and one might imagine a defence against them. It seemed, however, that a missile could not be shot down; suddenly the Soviets had the ultimate weapon in the combination of long-range missile and hydrogen bomb.

Once *Sputnik* had been launched, Americans had the sense that they were on the wrong side of a technological revolution. John F. Kennedy exploited this sense very effectively during the 1960 election, charging that the outgoing Eisenhower administration had allowed a missile gap to open between the two superpowers. The reality was different. Even in 1957 the United States had longer-range missiles, but Eisenhower had banned the use of military ones to launch the first (scientific) earth satellite.

Given the shock of *Sputnik*, the Eisenhower administration scrambled to find some way to give the European allies back their sense of security. One idea it hit upon was to give them shorter-range (intermediate-range) missiles – which were placed in Italy, Turkey and the United Kingdom. Until American ICBMs were operational, these weapons would offer a missile threat against the Soviet Union; but Eisenhower already knew that American bombers probably could penetrate Soviet air defences, so the missiles were more a matter of reassurance than of necessity. As it happened, the first US ICBMs became operational in September 1959. The

Wernher von Braun (1912–1977)

He began the era of long-range ballistic missiles by convincing the German army to develop them – to further his own ambition, he said, to put men into space. His wartime V-2 inspired the post-war ICBMs. At war's end von Braun surrendered to the US Army, for which he developed such missiles as Redstone (which launched the first US satellite). The Air Force having taken responsibility for longer-range missiles, von Braun moved to the new civilian NASA agency, for which he developed the Saturn rocket which put Americans on the moon.

shorter-range missiles became operational, in greater numbers, at about the same time.

The great irony was that, even some years later, with ICBMs rolling off US production lines, the Soviets still could not build ICBMs in any numbers, probably because they found it difficult to produce precise enough parts (shorter-range missiles were much less of a problem). The shorter-range weapons were a problem for Europeans but not for Americans – until and unless Khrushchev found some way of stationing such weapons closer to the United States.

The US ICBM

The rocket that could orbit a big satellite, could also carry an H-bomb from the Soviet Union to the United States, or vice versa. The Intercontinental Ballistic Missile (ICBM) typically could fly 5,000–10,000 miles (8,000–16,000 km); by the 1980s some such missiles could carry several warheads, placing each of them within 150 yards (137 m) of its target.

CHAPTER FIFTEEN

CUBA :

BAY OF PIGS

Two years after *Sputnik*, Americans suffered another shock. Fidel Castro overthrew the Cuban dictator, Fulgencio Batista. Initially few mourned Batista, but gradually it became clear that Castro was intent on creating a new Communist state only 90 miles (145 km) from Florida.

1959

1 January: Castro proclaims victory

1960

11 January: US formally protests Cuban seizures of US property

4 February: Castro negotiates trade agreements with the Soviets, first indication of his Communist leanings

8 July: United States suspends the Cuban sugar quota

16 August: First US assassination plot against Castro

1961

20 January: Kennedy inaugurated as President

12 April: Kennedy orders US forces not to become involved, cuts air support

14 April: Initial air strikes in support of the landing

17 April: Landing at Bay of Pigs; insurgents defeated

13 June: Kennedy orders other measures to deal with Castro

During the 1960 election, John F. Kennedy charged that the Eisenhower administration (against whose Vice President, Richard Nixon, he was running) had done nothing about Cuba. The US press praised Nixon, who was usually considered a virulent anti-Communist, for his restraint in opposing an invasion. Few knew that Nixon was silent because in March 1960 his administration had authorized planning the invasion Kennedy was demanding. Kennedy inherited the plan. The Eisenhower administration had used exiles recruited and backed by the CIA to overthrow the left-leaning Guatemalan government in 1954, and it planned to do much the same thing again.

Eisenhower had planned to use regular American forces to back up the exiles, but Kennedy feared that to do so would be to admit American involvement (Eisenhower later told him that it did not matter: any attempt to overthrow Castro would be seen as American). The plan was to land 1,500 Cubans. The landing place was originally Trinidad, near the Escambray Mountains, into which the attackers could fade in the event of some disaster. Under Kennedy the landing place was shifted to the Bay of Pigs, further west. Why is not clear. The 17 April 1961 attack failed disastrously, partly because Kennedy cancelled air support after

---

Fidel Castro (1926–2016)

Castro led a guerrilla army to victory in Cuba in 1959 after a six-year campaign. Once in power, he used resentment of Americans (who owned much of Cuban industry) as a way of maintaining it without allowing any sort of democracy. He tried to spark further Communist rebellions, first in Latin America and then in Africa. He relied heavily on the Soviets, and felt betrayed when Khrushchev withdrew  his missiles without bothering to consult him. His revolutionary activity in Africa may have been partly an attempt to make it impossible for the Soviets to sell him out during the era of détente.

---

the first strikes (landing in Florida, the pilots were unable to convince anyone that they were not working for the US government). Nor did the landing touch off the expected uprising among the Cubans, and there was no nearby refuge into which the attackers could withdraw to begin guerrilla warfare. US naval forces waiting offshore to support the landing were ordered not to intervene, and the Cubans smashed the exile force. Kennedy's role in the fiasco convinced Khrushchev that he lacked backbone.

Having failed to overthrow Castro, the United States imposed a

---

John F. Kennedy (1917-1963)

Charismatic and glamorous, he created an administration of unusual intellectual power. It included many of the new generation of strategists especially concerned with how to fight and survive in a nuclear world; Kennedy's special interest in counter-insurgency stemmed from his belief that the Soviets had adopted Third World revolution as a way to fight the Cold War without risking nuclear confrontation. As heir to the World War II leadership generation, Kennedy seems to have felt a special need to prove his mettle.

---

trade embargo which solidified Castro's existing ties with the Soviets. Khrushchev gained a potential base only 90 miles (145 km) from the United States. President Kennedy was left more determined than ever to prove that he could stand up to the Communists. Just before Kennedy's inauguration, Khrushchev had given a speech proclaiming his support for what he called "wars of national liberation". Kennedy saw it as an announcement that Khrushchev's new policy would be to attack the West in the Third World. For example, his Joint Chiefs of Staff thought that the Soviets were trying to seize the former Belgian Congo in Central Africa. In Kennedy's view, the most important role for the United States would be to squelch such rebellions, or, better, to adopt policies which would make them unnecessary. The failure at the Bay of Pigs seemed irrelevant; it was time to build American forces, particularly special forces, to take on the guerrillas Khrushchev had just announced he would support.

Castro, too, had proclaimed a mission of liberation, which seemed to be directed at Latin America, traditionally a US sphere of influence. Here Kennedy hoped to foment a social revolution which would make it unnecessary to use force: using the Alliance for Progress, envisaged as a Marshall Plan for Latin America. Meanwhile, many blamed the new President for the failure at the Bay of Pigs, and he certainly became determined to overthrow Castro, sponsoring a string of failed assassination plots.

CHAPTER SIXTEEN

THE

BERLIN WALL

**The German capital, 110 miles (175 km)
inside East Germany, was divided between
Allied (West) and Soviet (East) zones, but
the line between the two was open.**

1945

May: Four-power
occupation of
Berlin begins

1958

10 November:
Khrushchev
threatens to sign a
separate peace
with East Germany

1961

3 June: Khrushchev
meets Kennedy in
Vienna

13 August:
Construction of the
Wall begins

1963

26 June: Kennedy
visits Berlin: "Ich
bin ein Berliner"

1989

9 November: Wall
is torn down

By 1961 skilled East Germans were fleeing so quickly that a Russian joker suggested that soon only the hated ruler of the country, Walter Ulbricht, would be left. With so many engineers gone the East Germans had to cancel their major prestige project, a new jet airliner. Khrushchev refused either to bribe the East Germans to stay or to tolerate the collapse of East Germany. Considering West Berlin a relic of the temporary 1945 settlement. Khrushchev thought that a peace treaty would end its status. As the Western powers had no intention of leaving, Khrushchev, from November 1958, threatened to sign a peace with the East Germans and then expel the Westerners. The tiny garrison of West Berlin could not possibly rebuff the massive Soviet army. President Eisenhower considered all of this academic; nothing in Europe was worth risking the nuclear war that such an attack would probably cause. Periodically he sent his Secretary of State, John Foster Dulles, to declare that attacking West Berlin would cause nuclear war. Meetings about the status of the city were allowed to end inconclusively.

Taking office in January 1961, his successor, President Kennedy, was far less confident. He considered the lack of any real option short of nuclear war frightening rather than comforting. In February

Walter Ulbricht (1893–1973)

Ulbricht led East Germany from 1950 to 1971. A thorough Stalinist, he opposed the relaxation Stalin's heirs demanded, and felt vindicated when the (unfulfilled) promise of better conditions led to the 1953 uprising. He was the prime advocate of the Berlin Wall, and in 1968 he committed East German forces to help put down the Prague Spring – which he considered a direct threat to his own power. He was forced out because of his opposition to Willy Brandt's opening to East Germany.

Khrushchev announced that a peace treaty had to be signed before West German elections that autumn. When he met Kennedy in June, Khrushchev demanded a settlement by December. Kennedy announced that he would fight to hold West Berlin. Khrushchev noticed that Kennedy was not demanding continued access to the whole city. All that mattered was that West Berlin remain safe.

Khrushchev ordered the construction of a wall, about 100 miles long, to shut in East Berliners. Manned by 15,000 guards, it became the most potent symbol of the Cold War, splitting friend from friend, breaking up streets. East Germans tried to tunnel under the Wall or climb over it. In Len Deighton's novel *Funeral in Berlin*, later adapted for the cinema, funerals were used as cover for escapes (with the escapees inside coffins). Of about 10,000 East Germans who tried to cross the Wall, about half succeeded, and about 600 were shot while trying. With the Wall in place, the East German government was able to extort money from West Germany to allow elderly citizens out to join their families in the West, exchanging about 3.5 billion marks for 250,000 people.

CHAPTER SEVENTEEN

CUBAN MISSILE CRISIS

**Having survived Berlin,
President Kennedy faced a worse crisis
the following year.**

1945

February: Gagra conference: Khrushchev learns his ICBM programme is failing	10 August: CIA deduces that ballistic missiles are being sent to Cuba	7 September: Soviets deny the presence of ballistic missiles in Cuba	14 October: Photos clearly show ballistic missile bases being built in Cuba	24 October: Quarantine (blockade) begins.
24 May: Khrushchev orders secret missile deployment to Cuba	31 August: Republican charge in the Senate that Soviet rockets are in Cuba	15 September: First Soviet ballistic missiles arrive in Cuba	22 October: Kennedy announces presence of missiles in Cuba	28 October: Khrushchev agrees to withdraw missiles
				November: US missiles withdrawn from Turkey and Italy

Having survived Berlin, President Kennedy faced a worse crisis the following year. Khrushchev ordered medium- and intermediate-range nuclear missiles secretly placed in Cuba, a few minutes' flight time from the United States: 24 SS-4 launchers (36 missiles, range 1,100 nm) and 16 SS-5 launchers (24 missiles, range 2,400 nm), as well as defending fighters, surface-to-air missiles and surface weapons. US intelligence failed – inexplicably – to detect the arrival of the missiles. Presented in October with photographs showing the ballistic missile bases nearing completion, Kennedy reacted furiously. His advisers suggested attacking the missile sites before they became operational. US nuclear strike forces were placed on alert. When a Soviet anti-aircraft missile site in Cuba shot down a US U-2 photographing the island, there was talk of attacking its site. Nuclear war seemed imminent. Kennedy sought a less dangerous way to force the missiles out. He ordered a naval blockade of Cuba (which he called a quarantine, so that it was not formally an act of war). After a few very tense days and some careful diplomacy Khrushchev withdrew the missiles and promised never to base offensive weapons in Cuba.

Kennedy's administration believed (incorrectly, as it turned out) that the Soviets already had enough long-range ballistic missiles to destroy key cities in the United States. To the Soviets that made Kennedy's violent reaction proof that the Americans were unpredictable and dangerous; they had better be cautious lest they provoke war. Thus, during the Vietnam War, a few years later, the Soviets feared conflict intensifying to nuclear war (which was never remotely possible) until the United States agreed to peace talks in 1968. American intelligence never appreciated that the United States enjoyed this advantage.

Kennedy seems to have been reacting to American political realities – by October 1962 the mid-term Congressional campaign was well under way. As a Democrat, he felt vulnerable to Republican charges that he had ignored earlier information that missiles were being moved into Cuba. He had done so in July partly on the basis of Soviet assurances. Now the President felt betrayed and vulnerable.

Nor did the Americans understand why the missiles had been put into Cuba; they supposed that they offered the Soviets some special advantage, perhaps due to the very short time it would take a missile to reach Washington from Cuba. In fact, Khrushchev had learned that his ICBM programme was a shambles. He was inspired by the earlier deployment of US intermediate-range missiles to Turkey – which made up for delays in the American ICBM system. Khrushchev agreed to withdraw his missiles from Cuba only after Kennedy secretly agreed to withdraw US missiles from Turkey. To save Kennedy's face, the withdrawal from Turkey was announced long enough after the Soviet withdrawal so that that they did not seem related.

Khrushchev never consulted Castro when he agreed to withdraw the missiles: to the Soviets, he was no more independent than any of the puppet rulers of Eastern Europe. Castro feared that he might be abandoned altogether for some Soviet "accommodation" with the Americans. One way to make himself indispensable was to stay at the forefront of the "world revolution" the Soviets claimed to support. That may explain why it was the Cubans, not the Russians, who in the 1970s fought for African revolutionaries in Angola and Mozambique – a point not understood in the United States (where the Cubans were seen simply as Soviet proxies).

After the crisis, US intelligence gradually realized just how badly the Soviet long-range missile programme was going, and how vulnerable the existing ones were. The secret that the United States had an excellent chance of destroying the entire Soviet strategic strike system if it attacked first was known to the most senior officials of the Johnson and Nixon administrations. When the US advantage disappeared about 1969, President Nixon sought the first of the Cold War nuclear arms limitation agreements.

The Soviet SS-6 ICBM

This development was authorized in 1954; it first flew in 1957. It surprised US experts by being developed instead of a shorter-range MRBM; the trick was to group rocket engines (which might have powered the smaller missile) together to obtain enough thrust. The result was really too clumsy for a weapon, but it was and remains a very reliable space booster. At the time of the Cuban Missile Crisis, the entire Soviet long-range missile arsenal was probably four or five of these weapons.

In July 1945, the "Big Three" – Churchill, Truman and Stalin – met at Potsdam to work out details of the joint occupation of Germany, the guarantee being that nothing like World War II could happen again. The mood was very optimistic.

When American and Soviet troops met at the Elbe River in April 1945, Germany was finished – and it seemed that both countries would work together to maintain the peace.

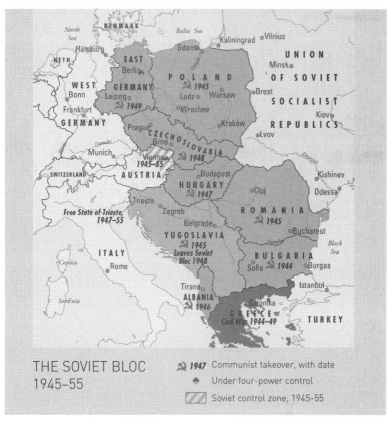

North Sea
DENMARK
Baltic Sea
Kaliningrad •Vilnius
Hamburg
Gdansk
NTH.
EAST
Berlin
POLAND
1945
Minsk•
UNION
OF SOVIET
WEST GERMANY
Bonn Leipzig 1949
Lodz Warsaw
•Brest
Frankfurt
Wroclaw
SOCIALIST
GERMANY
Prague CZECHOSLOVAKIA
Kraków
Kiev•
REPUBLICS
Danube Brno 1948
•Lvov
Munich Vienna 1945-55
AUSTRIA Budapest
Kishinev
SWITZERLAND
HUNGARY
1947
•Cluj
Odessa
Trieste
Zagreb
ROMANIA
1945
Free State of Trieste, 1947-55
Belgrade
•Bucharest
YUGOSLAVIA
1945
Danube
Black Sea
ITALY
Leaves Soviet Bloc 1948
BULGARIA
1944
•Corsica
Rome
Sofia
•Burgas
Tirana
Istanbul
Sardinia
ALBANIA
1946
Salonika
GREECE
Civil War 1944-49
TURKEY

THE SOVIET BLOC 1945-55

⚐ *1947* Communist takeover, with date

◆ Under four-power control

▨ Soviet control zone, 1945-55

Stalin rattled his big army, as in this 1947 May Day parade, and he began to talk tough, at least at home, telling Russians in February 1946 that their foreign enemies were still waiting to destroy them.

The division of Europe ran through two capitals, Berlin (seen here) and Vienna, each divided into four occupation zones, which were not, for the moment, closed off. Vienna (and Austria) would be neutralized in 1955, but Germany was the main running sore throughout the Cold War.

The United States rearmed Western Europe to help it stand up to the Soviets. The Western Europeans had the troops, but not the resources to provide them with modern weapons. These American-supplied medium tanks equipped the French 2nd Hussars Regiment, parading down the Champs Elysées on Bastille Day, 14 July 1954.

There really were a few Communist agents in the US government. For years belief in the guilt or innocence of Alger Hiss, a prominent Democrat accused by ex-Communist Whittaker Chambers, was a litmus test for American liberals. Here he is defending himself to a Federal Grand Jury in 1948. In the mid-1990s the release of decoded Soviet cables revealed that he had worked for Soviet naval intelligence, and that the Soviets had decorated him after the Yalta conference in 1945. The cables also showed that the number of such agents was far smaller than the overheated imaginations of the McCarthyists had envisaged.

McCarthyism actually predated McCarthy. These Hollywood stars, including Bogart and Lauren Bacall, marched to the Capitol for a hearing on Communist penetration of the Los Angeles film world, on 27 October 1947.

The mushroom cloud from "Grable", the first nuclear artillery shell, which was part of Operation Upshot-Knothole.

In the mid-1950s companies in the United States sold fallout shelters like this one, advertised in 1955. To the extent that they had a logic, it was that anyone living far enough from the blast of the bomb (for example, in a suburb) would be threatened only by the radioactive fallout, which would rain down for a few days at most. Cynics asked whether a family which had such a shelter would keep out neighbours who had not prepared one.

The atomic bomb dwarfed all previous weapons. The small objects visible on the white circle (actually a shock wave) are real warships, in the "Baker" (underwater) blast of the first post-1945 test series, at Bikini in July 1946.

The front cover from a 1963 nuclear attack protection booklet produced for homeowners by the British government.

In 1953, protesters in East Berlin could march directly into West Berlin via the Brandenburg Gate. When the Soviets crushed the rebellion in East Germany, West Berlin offered a haven – which would remain open for eight more years.

Guy Burgess fled to Moscow in 1951 with MacLean, apparently on the theory that if questioned MacLean would quickly reveal his espionage. He was a major Soviet agent, and also acted as cut-out for "Kim" Philby.

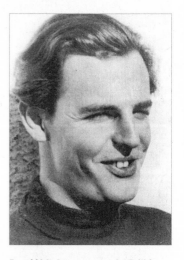

Donald MacLean was a senior British diplomat in 1951. Revealed by Anglo-American code-breaking, he and Guy Burgess fled to Moscow, making public the embarrassing existence of Soviet spies at the heart of the British establishment. He had been recruited as early as 1934 while at Oxford.

Yuri Gagarin became the first man in space on 12 April 1961, orbiting the earth before landing in Soviet desert.

Political disaster: few believed the Bay of Pigs had been anything but a US operation, despite President Kennedy's attempts to distance himself from it. Indian Communists march to the US Embassy in New Delhi on 21 April 1961.

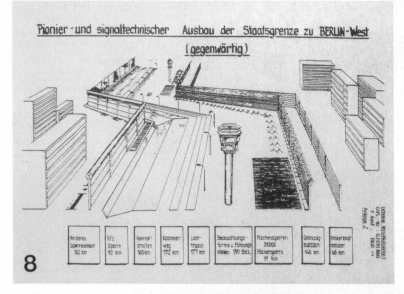

Classified Stasi document showing a cross-section of the Wall and listing
its specifications, including length (162 km/101 miles), watchtowers and
command posts (190) and anti-tank obstacles (38,000).

Soviet tanks occupied Prague, and some of the Czechs fought back. Most, however,
did not; perhaps they remembered how badly Budapest had been damaged.

Solidarity badge

Solidarity badge for
Gdańsk '81

Symbolic of all the East German regime feared and tried to suppress, an East
German punk helps destroy the Wall on 10 November 1989, the day after it fell.

The Wall is dead: Berliners, who can now be united, sit atop the Berlin Wall in front of the Brandenburg Gate, the symbol of their city.

On the wrong side of the military balance, Mikhail Gorbachev had to smile at President Reagan while the President assaulted him at the US–Soviet summit held in Reykjavík in October 1986.

To Yeltsin, the problem was, and had always been, the Party; despite the coup, Gorbachev thought that the Soviet Communist Party could still solve the country's problems. Here Yeltsin demands that Gorbachev resign as General Secretary of the Party, the post that previous Soviet rulers since Stalin had occupied.

CHAPTER EIGHTEEN

V I E T N A M

To Europeans, Vietnam did not seem
part of the Cold War. Americans argued
that while Vietnam itself might not be
vital, if it fell countries whose natural
resources really were vital to the West
would collapse: Thailand, Malaysia,
Burma and Indonesia.

1959

January: North
Vietnamese decide
to support armed
struggle in the
South

1961

October: President
Kennedy decides to
fight in South
Vietnam

1963

1 November: Coup
in South Vietnam;
Ngô Đình Diệm
killed

1965

8 March: First US
units (3rd Marines)
to South Vietnam

1968

31 January: Tet
Offensive

1972

30 March: North
Vietnamese begin
failed attack on
South Vietnam

1973

27 January: Peace
treaty ends Vietnam
War

29 March: Last US
troops leave South
Vietnam

1975

7 January: North
Vietnamese begin
successful offensive

30 April: North
Vietnamese occupy
Saigon

This "domino theory" was derided, but arguably the fight for South Vietnam bought time the other countries needed to become strong enough to survive.

The war grew out of the failed French attempt to regain their Indo-Chinese colony after the defeat of the Japanese in World War II. American reluctance to supply France (for what seemed at the time not to be part of the Cold War) embittered the French. After defeating the French at Dien Bien Phu, the Communists took over North Vietnam, but not South Vietnam or neighbouring Laos and Cambodia, which they still hoped to win.

By 1959 Communists in South Vietnam were losing their fight. They appealed to the North Vietnamese for help. As nominal head of the world Communist movement, Khrushchev vetoed such armed struggle for fear that it might touch off a nuclear holocaust. Given the split between Soviets and Chinese, the North Vietnamese did not feel bound by Khrushchev's order.

Ho Chí Minh (1890-1969)

Ho Chí Minh created Vietnam, initially leading rebels against the French. During World War II he fought the Japanese, and he thought he had secured an agreement from his American supporters that he would form an independent Vietnam afterwards. Negotiations with the French collapsed, beginning a war he won in 1954. Once in power, he brutally suppressed a peasant rebellion, to create a Communist state. By 1964 his control was complete enough to maintain order under the stress of a gruesome and lengthy war, the victory of which he did not live to see.

In 1963 President Kennedy's administration secretly sponsored a coup against South Vietnamese Premier Ngô Đình Diệm, who, it considered, was losing the war. That in effect made the US responsible for South Vietnam. Soon afterwards the North Vietnamese decided to send army units into South Vietnam to back up the assistance already provided. Fearing US retaliation, the North Vietnamese sought modern air defences. The Soviets, the only potential source, turned them down and withdrew their ambassador. However, using the threat that the rest of the world movement would see them as cowards, the North Vietnamese forced them to reverse course. Soon the Soviets were supplying the bulk of what North Vietnam needed, without gaining much control over the war. By this time Communist forces largely controlled Laos, funnelling supplies into South Vietnam through it and through Cambodia.

By 1965 US ground formations were fighting North Vietnamese troops and Viet Cong guerrillas. Fear of Chinese intervention (as in Korea) precluded any invasion of North Vietnam, the source of the war. The US government seemed not to be fighting the war wholeheartedly. Even the massive bombing campaign against North Vietnam was drastically limited. For example, anti-aircraft missile sites under construction could not be attacked for fear of killing the Chinese troops building them. For most of the war, attacks on the key harbour of Haiphong were barred for fear of sinking Soviet ships. Even so, at the peak of the war 500,000 US troops were in Vietnam; in all about 58,000 Americans died (47,000 in

Lyndon B. Johnson (1908–1973)

Johnson was a gifted politician caught in a war he did not want, unable to see any way out. His great wish was to effect social change in the United States, attacking racial discrimination and poverty. Thinking that war stemmed from a general desire for prosperity, in 1965 he tried to end the Vietnam War by offering a Mekong Delta development scheme. He turned against the war when, after it had put down the Tet Offensive, the US Army demanded 200,000 more men, suggesting that the war was unwinnable.

combat). The South Vietnamese forces lost 224,000; allies (South Korea, Thailand, Australia and New Zealand) lost another 5,300. The North Vietnamese/Viet Cong lost 1.1 million, but total deaths, including those in the North, may have been 4 million.

The war was frustrating for the Americans and the South Vietnamese; the enemy did not feel compelled to hold ground, but could melt away at will. Reports of corruption in South Vietnam and of incompetence in the South Vietnamese army, were deeply discouraging. A powerful anti-war movement in the United States arose; to some extent the North Vietnamese won their war in the United States.

In the 1968 Tet Offensive the Viet Cong finally risked what they hoped would be a decisive battle in the cities of South Vietnam, particularly the capital, Saigon, and the old imperial capital, Huê. They were badly beaten, but to many the extent of the offensive showed that the war was unwinnable. With the Viet Cong gone, however, much of the country was secured and the Americans began withdrawal. US and South Vietnamese forces defeated a 1972 North Vietnamese invasion across the Demilitarized Zone between the two countries. By then the US public saw little point in continuing the war. Congress imposed stronger and stronger restrictions on any further US involvement. When the North Vietnamese invaded again in 1975, this time through Laos and the Demilitarized Zone, Congress barred President Gerald Ford from helping. South Vietnam collapsed.

T H E　　P R A G U E　　S P R I N G

**By the mid-1960s the Central European
Communist countries were in serious
economic trouble because their political
orthodoxy overrode economic reality.**

1968

5 January:
Alexander Dubček
in power

23 March: Dubček
attends Warsaw
Pact meeting, tries
to reassure his
allies

5 May: Riots in
France

14 July: Warsaw
Pact meeting to
decide action

11 July: Article in
Pravda likens
Czechoslovak
democratization to
events in Hungary
in 1956

23 July: Soviets
announce large-
scale manoeuvres
(used as cover for
invasion)

20 August: Warsaw
Pact invades

29 August: Formal
announcement that
non-Communist
parties are now
barred

1969

17 April: Dubček
forced to resign

Decisions were geared to political demands and rewards, not efficiency. Worse, as an extension of the Soviet state, the Party concentrated on producing what the Soviet Union needed, and selling it to the Soviets, often well below the cost of production. Czechoslovakia had some of the worst problems because its Party boss, Antonín Novotný, was one of the most orthodox. In 1963 his country's national income declined for the first time in the Soviet bloc. Initially the Party resisted calls for reform by reducing central planning (i.e., the Party's control of the Czechoslovak economy). However, the problem was so obvious that the Party felt forced to appoint a new leader, Alexander Dubček, who was expected to limit reforms and so preserve the Party's power. Dubček soon realized that he had to open up the system to create "socialism with a human face". That face smiled on many of those who in other Communist countries would have been condemned. Emboldened Czechoslovak intellectuals and students demanded more radical changes. This was far more than the Party had bargained for. Worst of all, Czechoslovakia had an open border with Ukraine in the Soviet Union (and many Ukrainians could understand Czechoslovak radio broadcasts).

Communist bosses in the East European satellite countries complained to Moscow that their positions were being undermined. They found a willing listener in Leonid Brezhnev, who had succeeded Khrushchev after a 1964 coup. Demands by the East Europeans seem to have convinced a slightly hesitant Brezhnev to act. He proclaimed the "Brezhnev Doctrine": the Soviet Union would not stand by if Communism were threatened anywhere that it had taken root. He decided to invade Czechoslovakia to restore orthodox Communism.

Of the governments Brezhnev consulted, only Romania refused to participate (Brezhnev considered invading her, too). In effect, the Romanians withdrew from the Warsaw Pact, telling the Americans that they intended not to become involved in any Warsaw Pact attack, that they were not allowing Soviet nuclear weapons on their soil – and therefore that they hoped very much to be left out of any NATO nuclear targeting. The Romanians did retain formal membership in the Pact and they continued to receive new weapons (some of which they sold to Western intelligence).

Alexander Dubček (1921–1992)

He fought in the wartime underground and then rose through the Czech Communist Party to become First Secretary in 1968. Brought in to replace a Stalinist predecessor, he surprised his patrons by deciding that the problem was the Party itself, with its careerism and its rigidity. He was probably the most surprised of all that "socialism with a human face" was perceived as a great threat to every other country's orthodox Communism. Later he said that Brezhnev had deceived him by denying any intent to invade.

Attacking in August 1968, the combined Communist army of almost half a million met little overt resistance, although Czechoslovak radio stations and newspapers survived for about a week. Probably 83 were killed throughout the country, and several thousand were arrested. Having agreed not to resist, Dubček was allowed to stay in power. He was removed a year later after Czechoslovaks staged mass demonstrations nominally celebrating their defeat of a Soviet hockey team. Later he was expelled from the Czechoslovak Communist Party, but he was not imprisoned.

Western military experts were shocked by the invasion of Czechoslovakia. Preparations had been very successfully masked by a large training exercise. They had assumed that NATO would enjoy considerable warning of any Soviet-led attack. It would give NATO enough time to call up reserves, which were its real strength. Without those reserves, NATO could not counter a non-nuclear Soviet invasion. Was it now possible for the Soviets to attack suddenly, by surprise? To win without risking nuclear annihilation?

Paris Riots

In May 1968 Paris exploded in student riots. Due to the post-war baby boom and prosperity, an unprecedented number of students had to share grossly inadequate facilities. The students were also enraged that the French economy could not produce enough jobs for them. An attempt to put down the students brought on a general strike by Communist-led unions. The Communists then found that they had little power over union members, who rejected the deal that they extracted from the French government. Ultimately, the riots and the strike demonstrated just how fragile France was. The same divisions which had almost destroyed the state in 1946 (when a Communist rising seemed imminent) were still present. President de Gaulle survived the riots, but resigned less than a year later when reforms he advocated were not passed.

The Soviet Union suffered from many of the same problems as Czechoslovakia. What would happen if it chose a Dubček as its leader, and if there were no consortium of Communist armies to unseat him? In about 20 years the world found out.

In the West, the Soviet-led invasion attracted widespread attention and condemnation, particularly heightened, later, by the shocking self-immolation of the philosophy student Jan Palach in protest against his country's loss of freedom. The summer of 1968 also coincided with widespread student unrest in Western countries, including what looked like a revolution in Paris which began as a protest over students' living and working conditions.

CHAPTER TWENTY

DETENTE: PEAK
OF SOVIET POWER

**While the United States dissipated its
military resources in Vietnam, the Soviets
invested in new long-range missiles in
hardened silos, reversing the strategic
advantage Kennedy had enjoyed during
the Cuban crisis.**

1970

12 August: West
German non-
aggression pact
with Soviets
recognizes division
of Europe

1972

21 February: Nixon
visits China,
breaking enmity
between the two
countries

26 May: US and
Soviet Union sign
SALT I arms
limitation treaty
recognizing Soviet
numerical
superiority

22 November:
Helsinki conference
begins

1973

11 May: West
Germany
recognizes East
Germany

6 October: Middle
East War begins:
superpowers
co-operate to force
an end

1974

25 April: Coup in
Portugal opens up
last European
colonies in Africa

1975

1 August: Helsinki
final act recognizes
division of Europe

November:
Attempted pro-
Soviet coup in
Portugal

November: Cuban-
backed MPLA
proclaimed the
government of
Angola

In 1965 the United States had 934 ICBMs, mostly lightweight Minutemen, as well as 464 submarine-launched missiles. It estimated that the Soviets had 224 ICBMs and 107 very inferior submarine-launched weapons; even that situation was far better than what Khrushchev had faced in 1962. Late in President Richard Nixon's first year in office, 1969, the Soviets had 1,109 ICBMs; the US programme had ended at 1,054. Many of the Soviet missiles were huge SS-9s. All were in hardened silos, whereas the 1965 missiles had been vulnerable to a US first strike. The Soviets had 240 submarine-launched ballistic missiles, compared to 656 for the United States.

President Nixon felt compelled to maintain amicable relations with the Soviets even as they supplied weapons which were killing Americans in Vietnam. Uncomfortably aware of how dangerous the prospect of nuclear war had become, Nixon and his Soviet counterpart, Leonid Brezhnev, were both very careful not to let a Middle East war in 1973 (Israel against Egypt and Syria) intensify. Nixon's chief foreign policy adviser, Dr Henry Kissinger, called the new arrangement détente, meaning an easing of strained relations between the superpowers. That included signing the 1972 Strategic Arms Limitation Treaty (SALT), which seemed to ratify Soviet strategic superiority. Negotiations had begun soon after Nixon became President in 1969.

Many Europeans concluded that the Soviets no longer presented any threat, ignoring the less pleasant features of the Soviet system. It became popular to imagine that over time the two social systems might come to

Henry A. Kissinger (1923–)

Dr Kissinger first became prominent as a nuclear strategist. He was President Nixon's National Security Advisor and then Secretary of State, identified with the policy of détente (which conservatives considered far too accommodating) but also with the policy of escalation (to force a settlement) in Vietnam and also with the US attacks on Chile's Salvador Allende (which opponents argue was the cause of his fall). Liberals considered Kissinger far too cynical, and conservatives considered him far too willing to accept Soviet power.

resemble each other. Willy Brandt's West German government, pursuing a policy of Ostpolitik, formally recognized East Germany. That was a step towards the Soviet goal of having the West ratify their occupation of Eastern Europe. The necessary treaty, work on which had begun in 1972, was duly signed by 35 countries at Helsinki in 1975. The only Soviet concession, which they apparently regarded as laughable, was to accept a "basket" of human rights. However, in Eastern Europe the "Helsinki basket" inspired many to brave repression in the name of human rights, and this movement was ultimately very important in places such as Poland.

Willy Brandt (1913–1992)

Brandt created the policy of Ostpolitik: accommodation with the Soviets and East Germans in return for guaranteed security for West Germany and West Berlin. To do that he had to recognize the massive losses of territory to Poland and to the Soviet Union after World War II, which previous German governments had resisted. He was mayor of West Berlin, then German Foreign Minister, becoming Chancellor in 1969. Brandt was brought down in 1974 when his closest adviser, Günter Guillaume, was revealed as an East German spy.

The Soviets found that the West did not resist pro-Soviet coups and revolutions outside Europe – in countries which offered real advantages if they ever fought the West. Libya and Algeria provided bases on the Mediterranean. Angola and Mozambique lay athwart the tanker route around South Africa. Yemen could block the route through the Suez Canal. Angola and Mozambique offered sanctuary to guerrillas fighting in South Africa, the richest prize in Africa. Were they, too, Soviet proxies? We now know that in much of Africa the Soviets were concerned mainly to counter Chinese attempts to gain influence. Without an occupying army, Soviet control was limited. To Westerners, however, it seemed clear that the Soviet Union was the rising superpower.

Soviet success abroad masked serious domestic problems. To keep restive populations happy, they borrowed money to buy consumer goods from the West. Ostensibly the money would modernize industry, whose profits would pay back the loans. The problem was intractable because it was really political. The Party's managers often wasted their new machinery, while unpaid loans piled up. In 1981, for example, Poland needed to borrow $10–11 billion, of which $7–8 billion would pay interest on the existing outstanding loan. The Soviets gave Poland $4.5 billion in scarce hard (Western) currency that year merely to prevent the United States from using the loan request as a way of pressuring the Poles.

The Soviet Union suffered further because military production was swallowing so many resources. Yet its military leaders perceived a new kind of military weakness. By the late 1970s they perceived that the key to future war was the computer – which Western civilian industry was churning out, but which Soviet industry could not produce in quantity. Westerners, for whom computers were commonplace, could not imagine the extent to which the Soviet military sensed crisis.

Leonid Ilyich Brezhnev (1906–1982)

Brezhnev presided over the peak of Soviet power and the start of its demise in Afghanistan. Nicknamed the "ballerina" because he was "easy to turn", he came to power promising an end to Khrushchev's practice of suddenly starting and stopping ventures, thereby accepting all military programmes, whose growth strangled the Soviet Union. He regarded détente with the US as his personal achievement, and was proud of his relationship with President Nixon. He was personally responsible for the 1968 invasion of Czechoslovakia.

CHAPTER TWENTY - ONE

A F G H A N I S T A N

In 1978 a pro-Soviet coup overthrew the neutralist government of Afghanistan, on the southern Soviet border. The new government called on Moscow for help against rebelling Muslim tribesmen.

1978

27 April: Coup installs pro-Soviet government

1979

March: Afghan government asks for help to deal with rebels

12 December: Politburo authorizes intervention in "country A"

24 December: Soviets invade and overthrow existing Afghan government

1980

4 January: President Carter announces embargo on sales of technology to Soviet Union

1981

20 January: Ronald Reagan inaugurated as President

1985

March: Reagan orders increased lethal aid to Afghan rebels

1988

8 February: Soviets announce withdrawal (but continued support for the Afghan government)

1989

15 February: Last Soviet troops leave Afghanistan

1992

15 April: Soviet-backed Afghan government collapses

The Soviets feared that, if the government fell, an anti-Soviet successor might infect the Muslims of the southern Soviet Union with dangerous ideas. Given their Cold War mindset, it seemed (falsely) to the Soviets that the Afghan rebellion was being sponsored by the West. Just as the Americans had experienced in Vietnam, so the Soviets soon concluded that the government they were backing was ineffective. Surely a competent Afghan government backed by real (i.e., Soviet) troops would quickly deal with a few "medieval" tribesmen. In December 1979 the Soviets invaded Afghanistan with 25,000 troops and overthrew its government, installing a new one that they had chosen. Soon the Soviets had about 100,000 troops in the country. By the time the Soviets left in 1989, almost 14,000 (22,000 according to some sources) had died.

The invasion seemed to confirm the view in the West that the Soviet Union had never given up its aggressive attitude. Surely the Soviets had chosen to invade Afghanistan in order to realize the old Russian dream of access to the warm waters of the Arabian Sea and the Persian Gulf. It also seemed that the Afghan operation was connected to the roughly simultaneous Iranian revolution: Iran was an old Russian objective. That the Soviets had already been deeply involved in Afghanistan since the 1978 coup, and that they were in effect maintaining the same policy, went unremarked. In any case, the Soviets were now annexing Afghanistan, and they might well decide to push further.

Yuri V. Andropov (1914–1984)

He was Stalin's expeditor in Korea, and in 1954 became ambassador to Hungary, responsible for suppressing the 1956 rebellion. He was then put in charge of relations with other governing Communist parties, and in 1967 became chairman of the KGB. He led the fight to intervene in Afghanistan. Leaving the KGB, he became Central Committee Secretary for Ideology, then succeeded Brezhnev as Party leader. Once in office his main goal was to overcome the stagnation of the Brezhnev years, attacking alcoholism and absenteeism. Mikhail Gorbachev was his protégé.

American President Jimmy Carter, an advocate of further arms control and détente, changed course. Among other things he ordered the defence budget increased. The proposed SALT II arms control treaty was scrapped. The Americans boycotted the 1980 Moscow Olympics (the hosting of which was a matter of great pride to the Soviets) in protest against the invasion. Carter also approved American aid to the Afghan guerrillas resisting the Soviets, despite some fears that helping them would cause the Soviets to retaliate elsewhere.

Even before Western aid made itself felt, many in the Soviet government felt that the war was unwinnable. The guerrillas were effective and they refused to give up: the Soviets could not kill enough of them to extinguish their movement and they could not occupy the whole country – nor could they attack Pakistan, the guerrillas' main sanctuary and the immediate source of their arms. Failure was far worse than Vietnam had been for the Americans, because the Soviet empire (both inside and outside the Soviet Union) was held together by the threat of military force. If primitive tribesmen could defeat Soviet military power, surely others could, too. For the Politburo, the decisive argument against intervening in Poland was that it would be "Afghanistan in Europe" because, like the Afghans, the nationalistic Poles would surely fight. The Soviet situation in Afghanistan worsened drastically as, in the 1980s, the Americans (under Ronald Reagan) and the British (under Margaret Thatcher) greatly increased the level of aid to the guerrillas. In 1989 the Soviets felt compelled to withdraw their last troops, although they did continue to support the government they had installed in Kabul.

The Stinger Missile

It was one of many hand-launched infra-red guided anti-aircraft missiles which, from the Vietnam War onwards, made low altitudes very dangerous for aircraft. Such self-guided missiles provide a pilot with little or no warning. Aircraft therefore have to use counter-measures continuously, and they are armoured against the relatively small warhead a man-portable weapon can carry. Stingers supplied to the Afghan guerrillas effectively neutralized much of Soviet airpower. The current solution is for aircraft to rely on stand-off weapons.

CHAPTER TWENTY-TWO

DISSIDENTS

The Soviet state always feared that intellectuals like those who had created it would turn dissident and destroy it.

1961

Khrushchev's secret speech made public to press de-Stalinization

1962

Khrushchev approves publication of Solzhenitsyn's *One Day in the Life of Ivan Denisovich*

1964

14 October: Khrushchev ousted

Sakharov makes public appeal against revival of Stalinism

1966

14 February: Prison sentences for writers Andrei Sinyavsky and Yuli Daniel for publishing in the West

1969

Andrei Amalrik writes *Will the Soviet Union Survive to 1984?*

1974

13 February: Solzhenitsyn exiled after publishing *The Gulag Archipelago*

1977

1 January: Czechoslovak dissidents publish Charter 77 human rights manifesto

1 September: World Psychiatric Association censures Soviet use of psychiatric hospitals against dissidents

1980

January: Sakharov exiled to the closed city of Gorkiy

12 November: Amalrik killed in car crash in exile

The Soviet secret police, the KGB, deployed massive resources to detect those who refused to follow the Party's line. As in other police states, the KGB (and its equivalents in Eastern Europe) employed huge numbers of informers and wiretaps. To ensure loyalty, it secretly penetrated all official organizations (such as the military). It also tried to penetrate and thus to take over all dissident organizations, occasionally arresting their members. Such tactics were intended to convince anyone trying to form such a group that it was probably penetrated and therefore pointless. Contact with foreigners was particularly suspect. As an example of the scale of KGB operations, all visitors to the Soviet Union were followed and their telephones tapped as a matter of course. Stalin's regime relied largely on fear generated by random arrests and mass imprisonments, but such tactics were self-defeating. Stalin's successors almost immediately liberated most of the hundreds of thousands of political prisoners in Soviet concentration camps (gulags). Khrushchev went so far as to approve the publication of Aleksandr Solzhenitsyn's first novels describing Stalin's prison camps, *One Day in the Life of Ivan Denisovich* and *Cancer Ward*.

Aleksandr Solzhenitsyn (1918–2008)

Solzhenitsyn was imprisoned in 1945 for casual remarks about Stalin, then allowed by Khrushchev to publish his unprecedented first novel about life in a prison camp. His *Gulag Archipelago* trilogy described the vast Soviet prison camp system and the maniacally random way in which they were populated under Stalin. Solzhenitsyn's experiences convinced him that any sort of progressive ideology leads in the end to that kind of inhumanity; ultimately he attacked both the West and the Soviet Union for this sin. He was expelled from the Soviet Union in 1974.

For Khrushchev's successors, this was going much too far. Denunciation of Stalin risked questioning the basis of the Soviet state. Instead of recreating Stalin's terror, they developed a focused approach.

The KGB sought out and arrested individual dissidents. Those who refused to recant were often sent to mental hospitals, where they were in effect tortured (the Soviets were eventually expelled from the World Psychiatric Congress for this practice). The official justification for such treatment was that anyone opposing the Soviet state literally had to be insane, since there could be no escape from it. These tactics involved much smaller, though still quite significant, numbers than in Stalin's time. By 1985 there were 5,000–10,000 political prisoners in the Soviet Union, less than one per cent of Stalin's average.

The situation was further complicated by a new group of dissidents. After the 1967 Six Day War in the Middle East the Soviets broke off relations with Israel and began an anti-Semitic campaign within the Soviet Union. Soviet Jews tried to emigrate, but were blocked. They attracted foreign attention. In 1974 US Senator Henry Jackson managed to make trade relations (the Soviets needed American wheat) conditional on permitting Jews to emigrate, knowing that allowing any emigration at all would weaken the absolute control the Soviets felt they needed. This action infuriated those, like Dr Kissinger, seeking an accommodation with the Soviets. It showed other Soviet dissidents that their situation was not hopeless, because foreign pressure could be brought to bear on their government. For the Soviet authorities, this was more proof that it was vital to prevent contact between dissidents

Andrei D. Sakharov (1921–1989)

Sakharov invented the Soviet hydrogen bomb, then tried to convince his country's rulers that they should renounce nuclear tests; he considered such weapons far too devastating. His exalted scientific status allowed him to state openly what others could not, including outside publication. He was not permitted to travel to Stockholm to receive the 1975 Nobel Prize for peace, and in 1980 was exiled to the closed city of Gorkiy, specifically to prevent contact with foreign journalists. Many regarded him as the conscience of the dissident movement.

in the Soviet Union and Western media. Their existence and their words would be reported back into the Soviet Union by Western radio stations, which had a wide range of listeners despite official attempts to jam them. Thus the most prominent dissident to remain in the Soviet Union, Andrei Sakharov (who had invented the Soviet hydrogen bomb), was forced into internal exile in the closed city of Gorkiy.

The attempt to eliminate (or at least to contain) all dissidence failed. The dissidents never really threatened the Soviet regime, not least because all of their groups were so thoroughly penetrated; but the dissident movement built up habits of thought which would become very significant once controls had weakened, under Mikhail Gorbachev. Moreover, the dissidents created a widely read underground literature, *samizdat* (self-published). It included Andrei Amalrik's prophetic *Will the Soviet Union Survive to 1984?*. The Soviet dissident movement had equivalents throughout Soviet-dominated Eastern Europe, the difference being that in other countries it had the added support of nationalists who could not accept Soviet domination. Dissident movements such as the Czechoslovak Charter 77 (inspired by the Helsinki Accord) and the Polish Solidarity became their countries' governments when Soviet domination collapsed.

CHAPTER TWENTY-THREE

SOLIDARITY

**The Soviet empire in Eastern Europe
began in Poland at the end of World War II
in 1945 and it began to end there three
decades later.**

1970

14 December: Riots
in Gdańsk against
wage cuts;
Gomułka resigns

1976

25 June: Polish
government forced
by riots to withdraw
food price
increases

1978

16 October: Karol
Wojtyła becomes
Pope John Paul II

1980

14 August: Strike in
Gdańsk; Solidarity
Union formed

30 August: Polish
government allows
independent
unions; strike ends

14 December:
NATO warns
against Soviet
invasion of Poland

1981

18 September:
Soviets demand
crackdown on
Solidarity

13 December:
Martial law
declared in Poland

1982

13 March:
Solidarity, though
banned, stages a
large-scale march
in Gdańsk

1989

25 July: Having won
all the seats it
contested,
Solidarity refuses to
enter a coalition
with the
Communists

24 August: Polish
Communist
government voted
out of office

By that time the limited economic reforms begun after the 1956 crisis were no longer working. In 1976 the Polish government tried to raise prices. A wave of strikes followed, and the Polish government gave ground. Uniquely in the Soviet bloc, the government was unable to crush the workers. In 1980 the government again raised prices. Workers in the shipbuilding centre of Gdańsk went on strike. The yards there were a core Polish industry and, incidentally, a major resource for the Soviets (most Soviet amphibious ships came from Poland). The shipyard workers, led by Lech Wałęsa, formed a union, Solidarity, to defend themselves. Given the fiction that Communist states were run by and for their workers, an independent union was inconceivable. The union seemed poised not only to gain control of a major Polish industry, but also to spread its influence through the country. Solidarity promised not merely to break open Poland itself but also to inspire a similar movement in the Soviet Union. Such unions were among the worst Soviet nightmares: they were independent centres of power that could effectively defy the Party. Even worse, in the Polish case, the intellectuals the Party considered its property became involved with the union.

The Roman Catholic Church in Poland was already a source of dissidence. The Communists instinctively attacked organized religion as a possible rival for power, but Poland was heavily Roman Catholic and Poles associated the Church with Polish nationalism. Until the late 1970s the Roman Catholic Church sought accommodation with the Communist government. There was little point in martyrdom if that would not change the government. In 1978 a Pole, Karol Wojtyła, was elected Pope

---

Lech Wałęsa (1943–)

Wałęsa created Solidarity, which brought down the Communist regime in Poland. In 1976 he became spokesman for demonstrators at a Gdańsk shipyard protesting the erosion of the settlement to the 1970 riots. Fired, he joined the underground Workers' Self-Defence Committee. When a strike broke out in Gdańsk in 1980 he climbed a wall to take charge of what became Solidarity. The martial law designed to break Solidarity convinced Wałęsa that no settlement within the Communist system was possible; he became Poland's first post-Communist president.

John Paul II. He was a source of immense pride to Poles. Having lived under Nazi and Communist tyrannies, he refused to accept that Soviet rule would last forever. He sensed in Solidarity an opportunity for liberation. His Church supported Solidarity; some of its priests preached Polish nationalism rather than obedience to the Party. In 1981 an unsuccessful attempt was made on the Pope's life in Rome; many believed the Soviets were desperately trying to eliminate a mortal threat to their empire.

Within months of the formation of Solidarity, a majority of the Soviet Politburo wanted to invade Poland. As in Afghanistan, the existing government was proving unable to handle a serious challenge: it could not destroy the union. However, by late 1980 the Afghan adventure seemed far less attractive. Marshal Ogarkov, chief of the Soviet general staff, doubted that the Soviet Union could support two such wars at the same time. Although the Politburo actually approved an invasion plan in November 1980, Brezhnev backed off. Not only had he been warned off by the Americans, but it had become clear that the Poles would fight if they were invaded, given Polish hatred for the Russians and for the East Germans who would also have invaded. The Poles offered a solution: a military coup which would lead to martial law. The Minister of Defence, General Wojciech Jaruzelski, became Prime Minister in February 1981. By this time the combination of the Church and Solidarity was too strong to break. Through the 1980s Jaruzelski tried a combination of attacks and blandishments. As proof of his failure, in 1989 the Romanians tried to convince the other Warsaw Pact powers to invade Poland to break Solidarity, which had survived nearly a decade of Jaruzelski's attacks.

General Wojciech Jaruzelski (1923–2014)

He was Polish Minister of Defence when the 1980 Solidarity crisis erupted. He was made Prime Minister in the hope that he could solve the problem without requiring Soviet military intervention. Then he was made head of the Party – an unprecedented seizure of power by the uniformed military in a Communist country. Accused of tyranny, Jaruzelski had defended himself as a Polish patriot, protecting the country from the Soviet invasion which would have been inevitable had Solidarity not been fought from inside the country.

CHAPTER TWENTY-FOUR

PRESIDENT REAGAN'S

OFFENSIVE

To many Americans, the Soviet invasion of Afghanistan proved that the Soviets were on the march. There was a strong sense that the United States had allowed itself to fall much too far behind.

1979

3 May: Margaret Thatcher takes office

1981

20 January: Ronald Reagan inaugurated as President; Falklands War breaks out

1982

9 December: NATO foreign ministers vote to accept US Cruise and Pershing missiles

1983

25 October: Urgent Fury – US forces attack Grenada

1985

11 March: Gorbachev takes office

19 November: Geneva summit: Gorbachev meets Reagan (first US-Soviet summit since 1979)

1987

22 July: Gorbachev agrees to first cuts in nuclear weapons (abolition of medium-range weapons)

1989

20 January: Reagan leaves office

In 1980 Americans elected Ronald Reagan on an aggressive Cold War platform. He called the Soviets "the evil Empire". That went directly against the accepted wisdom, in Europe and in many quarters in the United States, that the Soviet Union was a permanent if unpleasant fact of life, which it was quixotic to resist. The Cold War was inherently unwinnable, the goal of statesmanship being to develop an acceptable accommodation with that reality. The West ought not to embarrass the Soviets with which it had to live. Reagan, however, made it clear, for example, that he did not regard Poland as an internal Soviet matter. He helped make sure that Poland would continue to be a running sore in the Soviet empire. To those unaware that the Cold War had been fought in the 1960s and 1970s in places such as Vietnam and Africa, it seemed that Reagan had begun a new Cold War.

Reagan saw the Soviets as weak, not secure; vigorous policies might force them to abandon the Cold War altogether. Defence costs were hurting Western economies badly enough; surely astronomical costs hit the Soviets far worse. Unknown to Americans, by this time the Soviet economy was actually contracting while it was increasing defence spending, an unsupportable situation.

Ronald Reagan (1911–2004)

Reagan won the Presidency promising to rearm to face the Soviets on equal terms; he did not expect the Cold War to end. However, his intelligence chief, William Casey, convinced him that the Soviets were in such great difficulties that negotiations and pressure from a position of strength might actually end the Cold War. It thus made sense to accept large (because temporary) budget deficits to build military strength. That could never be admitted, because if the Soviets realized that the build-up was temporary, they would wait it out.

Reagan's policies were designed to force the Soviets to spend even more on defence and so undermine their economy. He rebuilt American forces. Although he never said so, he seems to have justified the ruinous costs he ran on the grounds that they would end the Cold War altogether and so make it possible to cut defence spending in the long run – as actually happened. Very secret ("black") defence strategies were undertaken in hopes that their sudden disclosure would force the Soviets into crash programmes particularly destructive of their planned economy. Perhaps the most spectacular such programme was "Star Wars", the Strategic Defense Initiative (SDI) – an attempt to develop a defence against missile attack. Against the advice of Soviet scientists, the Soviet government sponsored an equivalent, the cost of which helped bankrupt it. It is still not clear to what extent, if any, the Reagan administration announced its programme with this end in mind.

Attacks on Soviet finances included making their loans more expensive and persuading the Saudis to cut the price of oil – since sales of Soviet oil were their major source of foreign exchange. Soviet oil production was declining as easily worked wells were exhausted. It would take more advanced – mainly American – technology to tap the much larger reserves still in the ground. President Reagan did his best to keep that out of Soviet hands. Reagan also tried to sabotage the Soviet project to sell piped natural gas to Western Europe, on the theory that the Europeans would come under Soviet control if they came to depend on Soviet gas for their energy.

Margaret Thatcher (1925–2013)

Thatcher became British Prime Minister in 1979 (the first woman premier in any major European country), remaining until 1990. She was instrumental in creating the decisive combination of keenness to "do business" with Mikhail Gorbachev without willingness to overlook Soviet misdeeds. Her decision to fight for the Falklands helped convince the Soviets that the West was not nearly so decadent as they had imagined. Her close relationship with US President Ronald Reagan was vital. Her success in reviving the British economy helped demonstrate that Capitalism had a future.

Like Khrushchev, Reagan announced support for wars of national liberation – against the Soviets and their proxies. That included backing the Afghan guerrillas and also Africans and Nicaraguans fighting Cubans and their proxies.

Margaret Thatcher, whose views were somewhat similar to Reagan's, had recently become British Prime Minister. She shared the President's view that there was no point in appeasing the Soviets. They became close friends and allies, strongly agreeing on what had to be done to save the West. Overall, Mrs Thatcher championed a vigorous foreign policy. Although her fight in the Falklands was not part of the Cold War, it had a dramatic effect on the Soviets, showing that they had failed altogether to destroy British national spirit.

CHAPTER TWENTY-FIVE

GORBACHEV: A MAN TO DO BUSINESS WITH

The Soviet Union entered the 1980s in crisis, its economy failing under the weight of enormous military programmes and Party incompetence.

1982

10 November: Brezhnev, long-time Soviet leader, dies

1984

9 February: Yuri Andropov, Brezhnev's successor, dies

1985

10 March: Konstantin Chernenko, Andropov's successor, dies

11 March: Gorbachev selected as next Soviet leader

1986

23 April: Gorbachev announces perestroika (restructuring)

16 May: Gorbachev announces anti-drinking policies

25 February: Gorbachev calls for radical economic reform

16 December: Andrei Sakharov released from internal exile

1989

26 March: Multi-party election for Soviet Duma (parliament)

Many Soviets had a sense that the country was in stagnation, that some change was badly needed. The elderly Leonid Brezhnev died in 1982, succeeded by the KGB's Yuri Andropov. Quite sick when he assumed power, Andropov died within two years, to be succeeded by the last of Brezhnev's generation, Konstantin Chernenko. He was clearly an interim choice, too sick to last long. Finally, in 1985 a man young enough to serve for years to come was chosen: Mikhail Gorbachev.

Gorbachev first met Ronald Reagan at Geneva in 1985, hoping to convince the President to cancel "Star Wars". Unfortunately he was not at all secure in his power – he needed the summit to prove his worth to the Politburo. The next year, at Reykjavik, Gorbachev tried to kill off the new intermediate-range missiles the United States was placing in Western Europe. Reagan extracted a ban on all such missiles on both sides. For the first time in the Cold War, an arms treaty, signed in 1987, actually reduced weapons on both sides. For Reagan, the lesson was clear: the only way to extract the desired cuts was to show determination in the face of Gorbachev's surprising weakness.

Gorbachev justified his election before the Politburo by promising to solve the crucial Soviet problem: military computer production. That was bound up with the larger Soviet economic problem.

Unlike Khrushchev (who had been ousted for doing so) Gorbachev could not simply order plants turning out other things, such as tanks or aircraft, to produce computers instead. He had to convince a generation of very cynical Soviet workers to work much harder, and to expand the economy sufficiently to add new industries. It took a few years for Gorbachev to discover much of what Dubček had sensed almost immediately in Czechoslovakia, facing a similar problem almost 20 years earlier.

Slogans, the staple of Soviet management, were not enough: workers had heard too many of them for far too long. Nor did it do much good to ban drinking during working hours or to arrest workers who stayed out of work to queue to buy scarce goods. Gorbachev hit on two new ideas not too different from Dubček's: *glasnost* (openness) and *perestroika* (restructuring). He would carry out perestroika by unleashing the creativity of Soviet citizens, promising them they would not be punished for speaking out of turn. The key guarantee

Mikhail Gorbachev (1931–)

Gorbachev had an unlikely background: his mentors were Yuri Andropov of the KGB and Mikhail Suslov, the reactionary ideologue of the Party. Both spent time in his district for kidney treatment. Once Andropov was in power, Gorbachev often acted as his deputy, but he was not the undisputed heir. Konstantin Ustinovich Chernenko was chosen as an interim leader, precisely because his short tenure would provide time for a longer-term choice. He was so feeble that Gorbachev often had to fill in for him, demonstrating his suitability as leader.

was glasnost: truth, rather than Party cant, would be honoured. Like any other upper-level Party official, Gorbachev assumed that, given the chance, workers would concentrate on making the Soviet Union more successful. Given years of misrule, the subject of free expression was too often the crimes of the Party.

Nor could Gorbachev fall back on the traditional Soviet alternative, repression. On the wrong side of the military balance, he badly needed détente. Unlike their predecessors, neither President Reagan nor Mrs Thatcher saw much point in a détente which would merely be a breathing space before the Soviets became aggressive again. To them the only guarantee of peace was transformation inside the Soviet Union. Gorbachev tried to outmanoeuvre his Western enemies by speaking directly to their populations, claiming (falsely) to cut military production and thus, in his words, undercutting them by removing the threat they cited. Although Gorbachev became popular in the West, this ploy failed.

Gorbachev gradually came to realize that the Party which had placed him in power was crippling the country. He therefore tried to cripple the Party, ending its monopoly on power. He never realized that the Party was also the sole mechanism which transmitted the ruler's orders to those who would carry them out. Without it, his new directives went nowhere. Stagnation was even worse than in Brezhnev's time. Gorbachev's tragedy was that he never understood his own political system well enough to develop any sort of viable replacement.

CHAPTER TWENTY-SIX

THE WALL

COMES DOWN

**The war in Afghanistan and the ongoing
political crisis in Poland seem to have
convinced Mikhail Gorbachev that the
East European empire could no longer be
held by force.**

1989

6 March: Soviets renounced Brezhnev doctrine in favour of "Sinatra Doctrine"

August: Ceaușescu of Romania demands that Warsaw Pact invade Poland to crush Solidarity

2 May: Hungarians begin opening their border to Austria

10 September: East German Neues Forum organization formed in East Berlin

11 September: First 10,000 East Germans arrive in West Germany via Hungary

7 October: Gorbachev visits East Germany

18 October: East German coup: Honecker replaced by Egon Krenz

4 November: East Germany's biggest demonstration: one million in East Berlin

9 November: East German borders opened; the Wall falls as guards stand by

28 November: West German Chancellor Helmut Kohl announces reunification plan

In 1988 he announced what became known as the "Sinatra Doctrine", named (in 1989) after the singer's signature song: "I'll Do It My Way". Never again would the Soviet Union impose its form of Communism on an Eastern European country by force. The Communist leaders of Eastern Europe vehemently disagreed, but Gorbachev had the troops. Now they were doomed, and they knew it. Gorbachev did not realize how devastating his decision was. He imagined that 40 years of Communist rule had produced a reasonably content population which would welcome a more relaxed version of Communism. Nor could he imagine just how vivid memories of Russian crimes, such as the suppression of Hungary in 1956 and the massacre of Poles at Katyn in 1940, were throughout Eastern Europe.

Hungary, led by Károly Grósz, was already the least conservative of the satellite countries. Given the "Sinatra Doctrine", in the summer of 1989 it decided to open its border to the West. Many Hungarians already travelled back and forth across the border, for example to trade in Austria. The radical step was that non-Hungarians might also cross. That in effect destroyed the Iron Curtain, because travel within the Communist bloc was relatively easy. That was acceptable only because the bloc as a whole was closed to the West. Letting East Germans through would destroy the East German regime: it would be like going back to the situation before the Wall. When the Hungarians asked Russian permission, they were told that, in accord with the new doctrine, what they did with their border was their own business.

Probably Gorbachev was pleased, because he feared that the remaining conservative rulers of Eastern Europe would provide havens for those Russians intent on overthrowing him. The most diehard of them all was Erich Honecker of East Germany. Visiting East Germany for the 40th anniversary of the state, Gorbachev publicly attacked Honecker for his unwillingness to reform. Sensing an opening, East Germans demonstrated in East Berlin, Dresden, Leipzig and other cities. Their Neues Forum organization had been formed about a month earlier in East Berlin. At first the Stasi attacked the crowds, but not hard enough to suppress the movement. By this time the East German economy was in crisis as a consequence of the mass exodus through

Hungary. These problems were used to justify what amounted to a Stasi coup against Honecker, who was replaced by the Stasi chief, Egon Krenz. Now the Stasi stood back, and a million people demonstrated in East Berlin. Even so, Gorbachev thought that the East German regime would continue as before. He imagined that ultimately a "liberalized" East Germany might join a confederation with West Germany, finally neutralizing that country.

Erich Honecker (1912–1994)

Honecker replaced Walter Ulbricht because he accepted the West German opening to the East (Ostpolitik), which the Soviets considered useful. That required greater repression in East Germany; otherwise the population might come to expect freedom. In 1980 Honecker demanded a Czech-style invasion to put down the Polish Solidarity movement. In 1988 he rejected glasnost and perestroika. By the time Mikhail Gorbachev was visiting him for the 40th anniversary of East Germany, a coup to unseat him was already well advanced.

Taking power, the new rulers suddenly discovered that East Germany was broke. Gorbachev had no hard currency to offer them, so they went to the West Germans, in the past always willing to provide enough to keep East Germany going. This time the West German Chancellor Helmut Kohl asked for moderate reforms such as easier terms for families in East Germany to rejoin their relatives in the West. The new East German government panicked: it officially gave up the Communist Party's monopoly on power. It also opened the Berlin Wall. With world media watching, an ecstatic crowd began to smash down the Wall. Kohl immediately put a reunification plan before the West German Bundestag. He soon manoeuvred Gorbachev into approving unification on his terms, Germany remaining in NATO. To the extent that the Cold War had been about the fate of Germany, Gorbachev had lost.

R E V O L U T I O N S   I N   E A S T E R N   E U R O P E

**To the orthodox Communist rulers of
Eastern Europe, Poland was a running
sore. Jaruzelski's failure to crush Solidarity
endangered all of them.**

1989

11 January:
Hungarian
government
commission
reverses official
claim that the 1956
revolution was a
foreign operation

18 February: Polish
government admits
that Soviets, not
Germans, carried
out the Katyn
Forest massacre

17 March: Huge
Hungarian
demonstrations
recall 1848 rising;
protest against
Communist
government

16 June: Imre Nagy
reburied with
honours: the
Hungarian
Revolution itself is
honoured

7 October:
Hungarian
Communist Party
abandons Leninism

28 October: Mass
demonstrations in
Prague crushed by
police

17 November:
Police attack
renewed
demonstrations in
Prague

24 November:
Czechoslovak
Communist
government resigns

Romanian
President Nicolae
Ceauşescu
confirmed in office

25 December:
Romanian
President Nicolae
Ceauşescu and his
wife are executed

In Hungary the government declared that in 1956 the Soviets had not put down a counter-revolution but, on the contrary, had crushed a legitimate government. In July 1989 Gorbachev shocked a Warsaw Pact meeting by supporting the Poles and the Hungarians. That August, Nicolae Ceauşescu of Romania demanded that the Pact invade Poland to crush Solidarity; he thought it was 1968 and that Poland was Czechoslovakia. Gorbachev, however, was not Brezhnev. The Poles were so contemptuous that they published Ceauşescu's letter.

Demonstrations alone probably would not have overthrown the remaining orthodox Communist governments. They still had powerful secret police and they had their own armies. Gorbachev, however, still feared that his Russian enemies would find refuges in the hard-line countries of Eastern Europe – which he now viewed as a net burden rather than an invaluable asset. Given his background working with the Soviet secret police, he had close ties with the secret police of the other Warsaw Pact countries, even those of the semi-estranged Romania.

Mass demonstrations began in Czechoslovakia a few days after the Wall collapsed in Berlin. Not only did the police not break them up, they

---

Václav Havel (1936–2011)

Havel was an absurdist playwright and philosopher before becoming involved in the Charter 77 movement. He was already in trouble for his unconventional writings, and given his continued underground activities he was imprisoned from time to time for his writings. His growing fame outside Czechoslovakia helped limit the sentences. Thus, sentenced to nine months in February 1989,
he was released after four. He led in the formation of the Civic Forum opposition group which replaced the Communist government of Czechoslovakia, and in January 1990 was chosen President.

---

seem to have encouraged them. The demonstrations were used within the Czechoslovak Party to justify a change of leadership. Gorbachev's intent was probably simply to replace the existing hard-line regime with a softer one, but the Czechoslovak population was having none of that. The Communist regime quickly yielded power to Václav Havel, who had long been a leader of the dissident Charter 77 movement.

Events at the end of 1989 in Romania were far more dramatic. Ceaușescu was the most obdurate of the Communist dictators. He was so intent on maintaining power that he forced all owners of typewriters to register samples of their output, so that any dissident letters could be

---

Nicolae Ceaușescu (1918–1989)

He became dictator of Romania in 1965, soon pursuing a somewhat independent policy (for example, his secret sales of Soviet hardware were important to Western intelligence agencies). As in East Germany, the flip side of a friendlier attitude to the West was more repression, for fear that the populace might expect some measure of freedom. Ceaușescu was unusually paranoid: his Securitate obtained typewriter samples so that they could run down dissidents. He also tried to create a ruling dynasty, which is why his wife was executed at his side.

---

traced to their authors! As in the other satellite states, the crisis began with huge demonstrations, triggered, in this case, by rumours. His own secret police brought Ceaușescu down, and, uniquely in the bloc, he and his wife were executed. This was more like what Gorbachev had in mind, in that the successor regime was really another Communist group (albeit nominally non-Communist). It lasted several more years.

Within a few months the empire Stalin had erected in Eastern Europe had crumbled. The people of countries absorbed into the Soviet Union itself still wanted out. Foremost among them were the three Baltic republics – Estonia, Latvia and Lithuania – which had been brought forcibly into the Soviet Union in 1940 as a result of the secret clauses of the treaty between Hitler and Stalin – clauses the existence of which the Soviet state had always denied (it claimed accession had been voluntary). Once the Communist Party gave up its statutory dominance, people in the Baltic states were free to elect parliaments which reflected their own desire for independence. For his part, Gorbachev found himself compelled to admit that Stalin's crimes had included seizing the three republics. Nevertheless, Gorbachev denounced declarations of independence by the Baltic states' parliaments, and sent in some troops. For example, in January 1991 they seized the television station in Vilnius, Lithuania, killing 13 people. However, Gorbachev could not afford full-scale suppression in the Baltic states, because he could not afford the rupture with the West that such action would have caused. The three Baltic republics were allowed to secede. It was up to Gorbachev to convince the elected governments of the other republics not to follow suit.

CHAPTER TWENTY-EIGHT

FALL OF THE SOVIET UNION

Gorbachev never saw himself as another Dubček. He thought that he was reforming the Soviet Union to save it, not sink it. Among his reforms were multi-candidate elections in the different republics making up the Soviet Union.

1988

16 November: Estonian republic (of Soviet Union) declares itself sovereign

1990

11 March: Lithuania declares independence

4 May: Latvia declares independence

23 November: Gorbachev announces a new Treaty of Union among the Soviet republics

1991

2–13 January: Soviet troops battle local nationalists in Vilnius, Lithuania

20 January: Soviet troops kill four in Riga, Latvia

19 August: Coup against Gorbachev

21 August: Coup collapses

1 December: Ukrainians vote for independence

25 December: Soviet flag hauled down for the last time

In some of them nationalists looked to the Baltic states and thought about their own full independence. Others were quite willing to remain in the Soviet Union, so long as they gained a measure of independence from Moscow. To Gorbachev, the solution was to turn the Soviet Union into a confederation bound by a new treaty.

To Gorbachev's enemies, the proposed treaty was the last straw. It had taken a remarkably long time for them to realize that, intentionally or not, Mikhail Gorbachev was destroying the system which had given them power. In August 1991 Gorbachev went on holiday by the Black Sea, planning to return to sign the treaty. His enemies deposed him in a coup led by Vice President Gennady I. Yanayev. The coup foundered, partly due to the courage shown by Boris Yeltsin, who had been elected President of the Russian Republic (within the Soviet Union). Yeltsin suddenly realized that he had greater legitimacy than Gorbachev, because he had actually been elected by popular vote, whereas Gorbachev had merely been appointed by the Communist Party's Politburo. It was Yeltsin who declared the coup illegal and then held out in Moscow, inside the Russian Republic parliament building (the so-called White House), and harangued besieging troops at their tanks.

Gorbachev was brought back into power – though a much-reduced power because of Yeltsin's rise. Yeltsin demanded that the Communist Party, which had organized the coup, be declared illegal. Gorbachev tried to negotiate a new treaty of union, but he failed. Among other problems, the Ukrainians did not want to be part of the same Soviet Union which had produced the Chernobyl nuclear accident and which, within living memory, had presided over mass killings and starvations in Ukraine in the 1930s. Without the treaty, the Soviet Union was dissolved in December 1991. A new Confederation of Independent States, including all of the former Soviet republics except for the three Baltic states, was created; the Russians tried to maintain control of defence and foreign affairs. In practice that attempt failed, and the different republics ultimately followed their own policies, much to the anger of many Russians.

With the breakup of the Soviet Union, the Cold War was finally over. The pressures the Soviet system had generated had been far too much for it; the one man who had tried to solve the system's problems had been unable to see beyond it to something viable.

The many consequences of the Cold War live on. Europe (at least outside Russia) is, as Ronald Reagan used to say, "whole and free", the former Soviet imperial states are now either in or about to join NATO and the European Union. That is a vast achievement. Whatever horrors terrorism by fundamentalists currently holds, with the end of the Cold War there is no longer a sense anywhere in the West that a thousand nuclear missiles can be launched on a dictator's whim. The world is no longer, at least for now, on the brink of destruction.

Boris Yeltsin (1931–2007)

Yeltsin learned just how exciting democracy could be when he began winning elections after Mikhail Gorbachev ejected him from a Party Central Committee position in 1987. He soon realized that elections gave him a legitimacy the Party – and Mikhail Gorbachev – lacked. As elected President of the Russian Federation (within the Soviet Union), he resisted the 1991 coup from within the Russian Federation building (the "White House") in Moscow, facing down the threat of attack by special forces. Later he demanded that the Communist Party, responsible for the coup, be banned.

However, the end of the Cold War has not ended the passions and ambitions that brought it about. The current Russian government would still like to regain some of the power it lost when its empire collapsed. Many of the former subjects of that empire are still resisting their pressures. The fight over the Ukrainian election of 2004 was only one of a long series of episodes. Russian troops are still fighting in what used to be Soviet Central Asia, among other things to protect the large Russian ethnic populations left there. Similarly, many in Moscow were furious when the three Baltic states joined NATO, bringing the old Cold War border onto their own territory.

There have been many indirect consequences, too. Yugoslavia disintegrated into war in the 1990s in large part because, with the collapse of the Soviet Union, there was no longer an external threat to hold that country together. The rebel success in Afghanistan undoubtedly convinced many in the Muslim world that Allah had blessed their movement, with consequences we see around us almost every day. The Cold War has ended. The War on Terrorism has begun.

INDEX

Page numbers in **bold** refer to main entries; page numbers in *italics* refer to illustrations/photographs/captions; page numbers in **_bold italic_** refer to timelines

C R E D I T S